Contents

Introduction

The Power Tips for Power Users Concept

Power users are people who know a program so well that they use it in the most efficient way possible. Especially in the case of DOS, they use it safely—avoiding shortcuts that could endanger their data. You can spot power users easily: they're the ones who finish their work while others are still struggling to get started. When something does go wrong with their system, they recover almost immediately and get back to normal. They're the ones other users approach when there's a problem.

More Than a Manual

Unlike many books of this type, Brady's *Power User's Pocket Guides* aren't designed as replacements for the user documentation shipped with a program. Instead, they are supplements to that documentation, intended to make you more productive by offering tips and shortcuts to make using the program easier, more productive, and safer. Microsoft decided with DOS 6 to cut back on the amount of material provided with the product. Instead, they provided the bulk of its documentation in an on-screen Help system that is little more than a command reference (and not a very thorough one). A supplement such as this book, therefore, is sorely needed.

This book helps you optimize your activities with DOS 6. It shows you how to select and use the most efficient and safest methods possible.

Working Task by Task

DOS 6's on-screen Help system is organized alphabetically by command, which is fine if you want to look up the syntax of the CHKDSK command. Where do you look to find out how to handle a Sector not found error, however? You will not find that information anywhere in the on-screen Help system.

This book, however, is organized with a task-by-task structure. If you need to recover data from a damaged disk, you will find all the information you need in one place. A complete index also helps you get at the information you need as fast as possible.

Don't get rid of your DOS manuals or the on-screen Help system; you will need them for detailed information on specific commands. This book suggests when you should look up the syntax of certain commands in the on-screen Help system. The small size and efficient organization of the *Power User's Pocket Guide* series makes it the quickest way to find the information you need.

Tip: If you just need a quick reminder of a DOS command's syntax, enter **FASTHELP** *command*, as in **FASTHELP CHKDSK**, instead of **HELP** *command*. The FASTHELP program provides a concise summary of command syntax, and it's much faster than HELP.

Who Should Read This Book?

All DOS 6 users will benefit from this book, even if they're not *advanced* users. Many people pay almost no attention to their operating system; they learn just enough to survive. They devote their energy to learning the one or two applications they use every day. Generally, that approach makes a lot of sense, but ignoring DOS can lead to problems. DOS includes facilities to protect and recover data, to optimize your system's memory use, to speed up your hard disk access times (which speeds up your entire system), and much, much more. If you ignore such facilities, you're not getting your money's worth from your system, and you could be endangering the reliability of your data.

If you know the basics of DOS—how to name a file, how to create a directory, how to change directories—you're ready to begin learning how to use it more efficiently and safely. Especially safely.

Where's DoubleSpace?

A few DOS facilities are too unreliable to use. You probably will not notice their absence in this book, but you may be expecting some advice on DOS 6's new data-compression facility, called *DoubleSpace.* I only have three words of advice: *Don't use it.* It already has developed a reputation for unreliability, and you don't want to take the chance of losing data from your hard disk. If you really need to double the amount of data stored on your hard disk, I suggest paying the extra money for one of the more reliable, third-party systems. Your software dealer should be able to help you select the one that is best for your system.

Part I

DOS SHELL AND THE COMMAND PROMPT

1

Power Tasks at the Command Prompt

Even if you use DOS Shell or Windows as your day-to-day interface with your system, you can do things at the command prompt that cannot be accomplished in any other way. DOS provides several power features when using the command prompt, such as redirecting input and output, creating DOSKEY macros, and creating a batch file from your command history.

Note: Many of the features discussed in this chapter require that the terminate-and-stay-resident (TSR) program DOSKEY is loaded. If you are not familiar with the basics of DOSKEY, look it up in DOS 6's Help system to see how to load the TSR, define macros, and access the command history.

Before You Do Anything Else

If you haven't already done so, you should make two emergency boot disks immediately. DOS 6 makes it much easier to boot from your hard disk even with problems, but you still can get into situations—such as complete hard disk failure—when you cannot boot at all from your hard disk. In that case, you'll need an emergency boot disk to start up your system so that you can restore the hard disk.

You'll need two floppy disks that fit your drive A. Use the
following steps to create each emergency boot disk. Don't use
DISKCOPY to create the second disk; DISKCOPY can sometimes produce inaccurate results. To make your emergency boot
disk, follow these steps:

1. Format a floppy disk using the /S switch to install the
   system files on it. If the disk has been used before, also
   include the /U switch to refresh the low-level formatting.

2. Copy the following files to the disk:

   FDISK.EXE

   FORMAT.COM

   SCANFIX.* (if you have DOS 6.2)

3. Label the disk and store it in a safe place.

Store each disk in a separate place so that if one disk is accidentally damaged, you still have the alternate.

Redirecting Input and Output

Note: See CTTY in DOS's on-screen Help system
for a command that permanently redirects all
keyboard input and monitor output to another
device.

Many of the DOS utilities, as well as some other programs, read
from the *standard input* device and write to the *standard output*
device. The DISKCOPY program, for example, sends the
message Copy another (Y/N)? to standard output, and then it
reads your answer from standard input. Usually, the standard
input device is the keyboard and the standard output device is
the monitor screen, but you can redirect these to other devices.
The symbols shown in table 1.1 redirect standard input or
output for only the current command; as soon as the command
is completed, the standard input and output devices return to
their normal locations.

Table 1.1. Redirection Symbols

Symbol	Function
>	Redirects standard output; if output if redirected to an existing file, the file is replaced.
>>	Redirects standard output; if output is redirected to an existing file, the redirected data is appended to the end of the file.
<	Redirects standard input.
|	Redirects the standard output of one program to the standard input of the next program (called *piping*); the | symbol must connect two commands on the same command line.

Not all the messages you see on your screen are directed to the standard output device, nor is all keyboard input read from the standard input device. Error messages such as `Bad command or file name` usually are directed to the *standard error output* device. Input and output for a third-party program may be read directly from the keyboard or sent directly to the monitor. Such input and output is not redirected by the symbols shown in table 1.1. As a simple example, suppose that you redirect the output of a DIR command, but the command results in the error message `File not found`. The `File not found` message appears on the monitor, even though the output of the command was redirected.

In addition, other types of input and output cannot be redirected using these symbols. DOS's COPY program, for example, reads from and writes to files or devices—not standard input and output; redirection symbols in a COPY command redirect standard messages (`1 File(s) copied`, for example), but not the data being copied. As another example, DOS's SET function reads no input and writes only to memory; you cannot redirect the input or the output of the SET command.

Keeping all these limitations in mind, what can you do with redirection? The next sections show you some effective redirection techniques.

Redirecting Output to a Device

Table 1.2 shows the device names that DOS recognizes. These names are used not only for redirection purposes, but also throughout DOS. You can turn your computer into a primitive (and very expensive) typewriter, for example, with the command COPY CON PRN, which copies data from the keyboard to the printer.

Table 1.2.   DOS Device Names

Name	Device
AUX	An auxiliary port.
COM1 through COM4	Serial (communications) ports 1 through 4.
CON	The computer console, comprising the keyboard and monitor unless it has been redirected by a CTTY command.
LPT1 through LPT3	Parallel (line printer) ports 1 through 3.
NUL	None; data redirected to NUL simply disappears.
PRN	The same as LPT1; DOS uses PRN as its standard printer for such functions as echo printing and screen printing.

The most common use for redirecting output to a device is to capture a hard copy of a program message. The following command, for example, documents the messages produced by the MEM command:

```
MEM > PRN
```

The following command documents the entire contents of drive C:

```
TREE /F > PRN
```

The command ECHO. sends a solo carriage return to standard output.

You can even use the ECHO command to add headings and explanations to the printout. ECHO writes its messages to the standard output device, and you can redirect them just like any other standard output. The following commands print the message, a blank line, and the directory listing:

```
ECHO   Contents of C:\BAT as of 5/10/94 > PRN
ECHO. > PRN
DIR C:\BAT > PRN
```

Redirecting data to the printer is a fast way of printing it, but DOS does not do any print formatting when you use this technique. There are no margins, no headers, and no page numbers. Wide lines may be wrapped or truncated, depending on your printer. Long messages will run right across the page break. The final or only page will not be ejected unless your printer ejects after a certain time lag, so the next thing you print may start on the same page. In general, except for short, narrow print jobs, you are better off using DOS's PRINT command, which does some formatting. PRINT's disadvantage, of course, is that it loads a TSR.

Power Tip: For many printers, you can eject the current page by sending a Ctrl+L signal to the printer. The command ECHO ^L > PRN will do it. (The expression ^L indicates that you pressed Ctrl+L on your keyboard; don't type ^ followed by L.)

Redirecting Output to NUL

Redirecting output to NUL simply suppresses the output. You may want to do this in a batch program for inexperienced users so that they don't have to cope with unexpected and unfamiliar messages.

Warning: Avoid redirecting input from NUL. The redirected program will wait forever for standard input; you will not be able to provide it from your keyboard. You must reboot to get out of the situation.

Redirecting Output to a New File

When you follow the > symbol with a filespec, the standard
output messages are written to the indicated file. If a file of that
name already exists, DOS replaces it with the new file. The
following command saves the current directory listing in
C:\MYDIR.SAV:

```
DIR > C:\MYDIR.SAV
```

Because all standard output is character data, MYDIR.SAV is a
vanilla text file that can be printed by PRINT, edited by EDIT,
displayed by TYPE, and handled by any program that deals with
text files.

Appending Output to an Existing File

If you want to append the current command's output to the end
of an existing file, you must use the >> symbol instead of just >.
The following command adds the current directory to the end of
the C:\MYDIR.SAV file:

```
DIR >> C:\MYDIR.SAV
```

The following set of commands creates (or replaces) a file named
MEMSAV, stores a message at the beginning of it, and adds
MEM output after a blank line. The first command uses > so
that any existing MEMSAV file is replaced. The next two
commands use >> so that their output is appended to the new
file instead of replacing it:

```
ECHO MEM results on 5/10/94 > C:\MEMSAV
ECHO. >> C:\MEMSAV
MEM /D >> MEMSAV
```

Redirecting MORE and SORT

Two DOS commands almost beg to be redirected: MORE and
SORT. MORE reads lines from the standard input device,
breaks them into pages, and displays them one page at a time on
the standard output device. SORT reads a file from standard
input, sorts it, and writes the sorted file to standard output.

Displaying Pages of Text

The MORE command becomes useful when you redirect its standard input from a text file. The following command displays the file named C:\MYDIR.SAV, one page at a time:

```
MORE < C:\MYDIR.SAV
```

People often pipe long output messages to MORE. Using the TREE command with the /F switch, for example, can produce several pages of information. If you don't pause it somehow, you can read only the last page. The following command displays the output of TREE /F, one page at a time:

```
TREE /F ¦ MORE
```

Sorting Files

SORT becomes most useful when you redirect both its input and its output to files or devices. The following command sorts the file MYLIST and prints the result (MYLIST is unchanged):

```
SORT < MYLIST > PRN
```

The following command sorts MYLIST and stores the result in SORTLIST (MYLIST is unchanged):

```
SORT < MYLIST > SORTLIST
```

Dealing with Temporary Pipe Files

Piping works by writing the standard output of the first program to temporary disk files, and then reading the standard input of the second program from the same files. DOS erases the temporary files after the second program reads them. If a great deal of data is being piped, you will notice a delay while DOS writes it to the disk.

Note: Environment variables are explained in Chapter 11.

If the DOS environment defines a variable named TEMP, DOS writes the temporary files to the drive and directory specified by TEMP. If TEMP is not defined or does not identify a valid directory, DOS writes the temporary files in the current directory. In either case, if DOS cannot write the temporary files for any reason (the disk is full or write-protected, for example), the command fails. If your setup currently does not define TEMP, you should add an appropriate SET command to AUTOEXEC.BAT, because DOS uses TEMP for all its temporary files, not just for piping (and so does Windows). The following command establishes C:\TEMPY as the directory for temporary files:

```
SET TEMP=C:\TEMPY
```

DOS does not create C:\TEMPY automatically; you must create it yourself before DOS can use it.

Ordinarily, you will never see a temporary piping file on your drive. But if DOS is interrupted before it can delete the temporary files (by a power outage, perhaps), the files are abandoned and you will have to delete them manually. Look for two files named something like AJCJTMBL and AJCJRCFS. You also may see the temporary piping files if you switch tasks before DOS can delete them and list the directory from the new task.

Power Tip: Any operation that uses TEMP runs significantly faster if you direct TEMP to a RAM drive. Be sure to put the RAM drive in extended or expanded memory so that you don't take up valuable conventional memory space. If you use Windows, the RAM drive must be at least 2M in order to accommodate Windows' temporary print files.

Combining Commands

When DOSKEY is present, you can combine two or more commands on one command line by pressing Ctrl+T between commands. Ctrl+T produces the symbol ¶ on-screen. The following command line lists all EXE and COM files on the current drive in alphabetical order by directory and file name:

```
DIR \*.EXE /S /B > \TEMPDIR ¶ DIR \*.COM /S /B >>
TEMPDIR ¶ SORT < TEMPDIR ¦ MORE ¶ DEL \TEMPDIR
```

First, this command line stores a listing of all EXE files in a new file named TEMPDIR. Next, it adds the listing of all COM files to TEMPDIR. Then, it sorts TEMPDIR and displays the result in pages. Finally, it deletes TEMPDIR.

These four commands could be entered separately, of course. The overall result would be the same; in fact, DOSKEY passes the commands to DOS one at a time. (You see on your screen each individual command being processed by DOS.) Combining these commands makes a big difference in your DOSKEY command history, however. The entire command line comprises only one entry in the history and can be recalled as a whole. Thus, you could repeat this procedure over and over again by simply recalling one entry from the command history. And you can easily turn it into a DOSKEY macro, as you see a little later in this chapter.

Some people feel that combining commands establishes some kind of logical connection between them. This is not the case; there is no connection between combined commands except those that you intentionally create using techniques such as temporary files. The following list is more specific:

- The output from one command is not automatically piped to the next one. That is why TEMPDIR was needed in the example.

- The execution of an individual command does not depend on the success of the preceding ones; if one command fails due to some kind of error, the next command is executed anyway.

- Piping and redirection apply only to the individual command they appear in. In the example, the first command redirects only its output to TEMPDIR. The second command redirects only its output to TEMPDIR, using >> instead of > so that the data is appended to TEMPDIR. The third command redirects only the input for the SORT command from TEMPDIR and pipes only the output of the SORT command to MORE.

You cannot go wrong if you remember that DOS receives and processes each individual command separately.

Using the Command History

Note: In the DOS 6 Help system, check the DOSKEY--Notes section for a list of keys that access DOSKEY's command history by typing **Help DOSKEY--Notes**. Ignore F1 through F6, which have nothing to do with the command history.

When you first use DOSKEY, you quickly learn to press the up-arrow key to recall former commands. Many people never learn any more techniques, but when you need to go back more than a couple of commands, DOSKEY offers several methods that are faster:

- Pressing the PgUp key moves to the beginning of the command history, and pressing the down-arrow key moves forward through the list. (Pressing PgDn moves to the end of the list.)

- Often the fastest way to recall a command is to type its first few characters and press F8. If you get a different command, keep pressing F8 until you reach the command you want.

- Pressing F7 displays a numbered list of all the commands in the history (see fig. 1.1). You then can press F9 to display the prompt Line number. Enter the number of the command you want.

```
C:\>
1: x
2: cd \
3: dir a:
4: dir a: | find "BAT"
5: MD C:\TEMPBAT
6: XCOPY A:*.BAT C:TEMPBAT
7: DIR C:\TEMPBAT
8: CLS
C:\>Line number:
```

Figure 1.1. *When DOSKEY is installed, pressing F7 displays a numbered command list (shown after the first command prompt). Pressing F9 prompts for a command number (shown at the second command prompt).*

If the list produced by the F7 key is longer than the number of lines on your screen, DOSKEY pages it automatically. You cannot redirect the output of F7 to print because there is no opportunity to enter a redirection symbol, but you can use the DOSKEY /H command to display a similar list, without numbers, that can be redirected. Or you can press the Print Screen key to print the list that is currently on-screen.

Note: When DOSKEY's buffer is full, each command you enter displaces the oldest command in the buffer, causing all preceding commands to be renumbered. So command number 14 now is not necessarily command number 14 two minutes from now. The default-sized buffer holds about 50 commands.

Turning a Command into a DOSKEY Macro

If you find yourself recalling the same command repeatedly, why not make it into a macro? It will be much easier to recall. All you have to do is recall the command, press Home to place the cursor at the beginning, press Ins to turn on insert mode, type **DOSKEY** *macroname=*, and press Enter.

Creating a Batch File from the DOSKEY Buffer

You can easily create a batch file from your command history by redirecting the output of the DOSKEY /H command to a BAT file. The following command, for example, stores the current command history in a file named REMARK.BAT:

```
DOSKEY /H > REMARK.BAT
```

You then may want to edit REMARK.BAT to add ECHO and REM commands, replace filespecs with replaceable parameters, remove unwanted commands, and so on.

Power Tip: Press Alt+F7 to clear the command history before entering a series of commands that you intend to save in a batch file.

Similarly, you can create a batch program out of your current set of macros by redirecting the output of the DOSKEY /M command, and then editing the resulting file. The stored macros take this form:

```
macroname=commandline
```

If you want the batch program to execute the commands contained in the command lines, delete *macroname=* so that each line is a valid DOS command. You also will need to separate combined commands; the batch processor does not recognize the command separator symbol. If you want the batch program to define the same set of macros, don't delete *macroname=*. Instead, add DOSKEY to the beginning of each line to create valid DOSKEY commands to define the macros.

Setting Up a Batch File to Create Your Macros

Suppose that you want to work with the same set of DOSKEY macros whenever you are using DOS. Define the macros once, turn them into a batch file that defines the macros, and call that batch file from AUTOEXEC.BAT. If the file is named MYMACROS.BAT, for example, you would insert this line in AUTOEXEC.BAT:

```
CALL C:\BATCHES\MYMACROS
```

Unless MYMACROS is in the boot directory, put the CALL command after the PATH command or include a path in it, as shown here.

Using Special Codes when Defining DOSKEY Macros

Note: In the DOS 6 Help system, check DOSKEY--Notes for a list of special codes you can use in macro definitions.

You often will need to include special symbols for piping, redirection, and combined commands when creating a macro. But if you include symbols such as |, >, or ¶ in the DOSKEY *macroname* = command, DOS executes them on the spot, causing an incorrect macro definition and often a DOS syntax error as well. You need to replace the normal DOS symbols with special DOSKEY codes. The following command, for example, turns the combined command discussed previously into a DOSKEY macro:

```
DOSKEY LISTER=DIR \*.EXE /S /B $G \TEMPDIR $T DIR
\*.COM /S /B $G$G TEMPDIR $T SORT $L TEMPDIR $B MORE
$T DEL \TEMPDIR
```

Note: The PAUSE command works well in DOSKEY macros and gives you time to read the output of one command before executing the next command. ECHO OFF does not work as well; it suppresses the command prompt but not the command itself. If you decide to turn off ECHO, be sure to turn it back on, or all future command prompts are suppressed.

Inserting Replaceable Parameters in DOSKEY Macros

You can use $1 through $9 to insert variable parameters in DOSKEY macros, much as %1 through %9 represent parameters in batch files. The LISTER macro, defined at the end of the preceding section, could be more generally useful if you replace *.EXE and *.DIR with $1 and $2. Include specific parameters when you execute the macro. The following command uses the revised LISTER macro to produce a sorted and paged listing of all DOC and BAK files on the current drive:

```
LISTER *.DOC *.BAK
```

DOSKEY also makes available the $* variable, which is replaced by all parameters from the invoking command. Suppose that you want to create a simple PDIR macro to print a directory listing. If you use the $* parameter instead of $1, you can include DIR switches when you call the macro. The macro definition looks like this:

```
DOSKEY PDIR=DIR $* $G PRN
```

The following command uses PDIR to print a listing of all files in the current directory:

```
PDIR *.*
```

The following command uses PDIR to print a listing of all BAK files on drive C, sorted by size:

```
PDIR C:\*.BAK /S /OS
```

All three parameters replace the $*, so the command that is passed to DOS looks like this:

```
DIR C:\*.BAK /S /OS > PRN
```

Note: Chapter 3 discusses the FOR command in detail.

You can combine $* with FOR to provide multiple filespecs for commands that normally recognize only one—such as DIR, DEL, XCOPY, and PRINT. The following command, for example, copies four sets of files from the current directory to drive A:

```
FOR %F IN (*.DOC *.DOT *.TIF *.PCS) DO XCOPY %F A:
```

You can turn this command into a macro that copies any number of file sets to A:

```
DOSKEY MCOPY=FOR %F IN ($*) DO XCOPY %F A:
```

Now you can copy the previous four sets of files with the following command:

```
MCOPY *.DOC *.DOT *.TIF *.PCX
```

Similarly, you can create a macro that prints multiple sets of files:

```
DOSKEY MPRINT=FOR %F IN ($*) DO PRINT %F
```

The following macro enables you to specify multiple filespecs to be deleted:

```
DOSKEY MDEL=FOR %F IN ($*) DO DEL %F
```

Using DOSKEY Macros to Inhibit Other Commands

When you enter a command, DOSKEY looks at it before DOS does. If it is a DOSKEY macro, DOSKEY interprets it, passing commands to DOS as necessary. Because DOSKEY gets there first, you can use DOSKEY macros to inhibit normal DOS commands. If you define a macro named DIR, for example, any subsequent command starting with DIR invokes the macro instead of DOS's DIR command; in effect, you replace DOS's DIR command with one of your own.

You can use this feature to disable certain commands that you don't want people to use on your computer, such as RECOVER or APPEND. You can replace the RECOVER command with a message by defining a macro this way:

```
DOSKEY RECOVER=ECHO PLEASE SEE N. LEIGH BEFORE USING
THIS COMMAND
```

Another reason to replace a DOS command is to insert certain switches and parameters into the command. The DEL command, for example, offers a /P switch that causes each file name to be listed for confirmation before deletion. The following macro forces the /P switch to be used with every DEL command:

```
DOSKEY DEL=DEL $* /P
```

Note: The order of the parameters is important in this particular example because, with DEL, /P must follow the filespec.

Replacing Standard DOS Commands with Macros

You also can use DOSKEY's macro feature to replace commands such as DEL, PRINT, and XCOPY with commands that accept multiple filespecs. The macros named MDEL, MPRINT, and MCOPY, presented earlier, could as easily be named DEL, PRINT, and XCOPY so that they would replace DOS's usual DEL, PRINT, and XCOPY commands.

Bypassing DOSKEY Macros

If you do set up macros to replace DOS's normal commands, you occasionally may want to access the regular command. If you inhibit the RECOVER command, for example, you still can use RECOVER to rescue files. Whenever you enter a command that starts with one or more spaces, DOSKEY ignores it; the command is processed by DOS. So to bypass the DOSKEY macro and reach the real RECOVER command, type one or more spaces at the beginning of the command line, and then type the desired RECOVER command.

Increasing Your DOSKEY Buffer

If you don't define any macros, the default DOSKEY buffer (512 bytes) is large enough to hold approximately 50 commands, depending on the number of characters in each command, of course. But each macro you define steals space away from the command history. In fact, a macro may overwrite one or more commands in the history, not necessarily at the beginning of the history, cutting the history short. You can fill approximately half the buffer with macros; the other half is reserved for the command history. If you exceed the space permitted for macros, you see the message `Insufficient memory to store macro. Use the DOSKEY command with the /BUFSIZE switch to increase available memory.`

The following command installs DOSKEY with a 2M buffer, but only if it hasn't already been installed:

```
DOSKEY /BUFSIZE=2048
```

You cannot change the size of the buffer without reinstalling DOSKEY, which clears your macros and command history. You can add the /BUFSIZE switch to the DOSKEY command in AUTOEXEC.BAT and reboot, or you can use the /REINSTALL switch with /BUFSIZE to install a new copy of DOSKEY and a new buffer without rebooting. /REINSTALL causes the old copy of DOSKEY and its buffer to be abandoned in memory, which wastes some space.

2

Tailoring the Command Prompt Interface

You really don't have to live with the plain old black-and-white DOS command prompt screen. You can do several things to add more interesting information, graphics, and color to the screen. You can even redefine the keys on your keyboard to tailor them to your work needs.

Dressing Up the Command Prompt, Part 1

This comes as a surprise to many people, but DOS's default command prompt is simply the current drive letter followed by a right angle bracket, as in C>. No colon, no path. This is a leftover from the earliest DOS days when there were no hard drives or paths; all you really needed to know was whether you were on drive A or B.

Nowadays, DOS's installation program inserts in your AUTOEXEC.BAT file the following PROMPT command, which sets up the standard prompt we are all used to—the current path followed by a right angle bracket. This is the prompt that most people want:

```
PROMPT $P$G
```

> **Note:** Look up PROMPT in DOS's on-screen
> Help program to see a list of special codes that you
> can use in the PROMPT command.

But you can do much more with the PROMPT command. You
can add your own text and insert system information, such as the
date and time. When you use PROMPT with ANSI.SYS (as you
see later in this chapter), you can redesign the entire command
prompt screen. The following list shows sample PROMPT
commands on the left and the resulting command prompt on
the right:

```
PROMPT Date: $D$E$E$E$G              Date: Tue 03-
                                     04-2001===>

PROMPT Your wish is my command...    Your wish is
                                     my command...

PROMPT $V$_$P$G                      MS-DOS
                                     Version 6.20

                                     C:\>
```

Notice that you have to use special exception codes for certain
characters. You cannot use the > character for a right angle
bracket, for example, because that character redirects the output
of the PROMPT command. So you have to use $G. (The *G*
stands for *greater than.*) In the last example, the $_ code starts
a new line.

The $H code deletes the preceding character on the line. It
comes in handiest to delete trailing information from the system
date and time. The following command displays the date
without the year on line 1, the time to the nearest minute on line
2, and the standard prompt on line 3, as shown in the example
that follows it:

```
PROMPT $D$H$H$H$H$H$_$T$H$H$H$H$H$H$_$P$G

Tue 06-18
3:15
C:\>
```

Adding Graphics to the Screen

In personal computers, character data is stored and transmitted using ASCII, which uses seven bits to represent each character. With seven bits, you can represent 128 different characters, but not all of them are standardized by ASCII. If you think of each combination of bits as a decimal number, from 0 to 127, the combinations from 32 through 126 are standardized; 32 represents a space, 33 represents an exclamation point (!), and so on. In addition, 8, 9, 10, and 13 represent a backspace, tab, linefeed, and carriage return. 0 is treated as a null character. The other characters from 1 to 31 originally represented control signals for transmitting data via teletype: start-of-text, end-of-text, and so on. These characters are not needed with personal computers; some PC programs use them for other purposes; others simply ignore them.

Microcomputers have an eight-bit byte, and with ASCII's basic code system, the eighth bit goes to waste. Programmers began using it to extend the character set, because with eight bits, you can represent another 128 characters. This extended set of characters has never been standardized and varies from program to program. DOS interprets the extended characters as shown in table 2.1. You can use these characters on the command prompt screen. (Many other programs also recognize the same character set.)

Table 2.1.   The ASCII Extended Character Set

No. /Character	No. /Character	No. /Character
128 Ç	139 ï	150 û
129 ü	140 î	151 ù
130 é	141 ì	152 ÿ
131 â	142 Ä	153 Ö
132 ä	143 Å	154 Ü
133 à	144 É	155 ¢
134 å	145 æ	156 £
135 ç	146 Æ	157 ¥
136 ê	147 ô	158 ℞
137 ë	148 ö	159 ƒ
138 è	149 ò	160 á

continues

Table 2.1.   Continued

No. /Character	No. /Character	No. /Character
161 í	200 ⌐	239 ∩
162 ó	201 ╔	240 ≡
163 ú	202 ╩	241 ±
164 ñ	203 ╦	242 ≥
165 Ñ	204 ╠	243 ≤
166 ª	205 =	244 ⌠
167 º	206 ╬	245 ⌡
168 ¿	207 ╧	246 ÷
169 ⌐	208 ╨	247 ≈
170 ¬	209 ╤	248 °
171 ½	210 ╥	249 ·
172 ¼	211 ╙	250 ·
173 ¡	212 ╘	251 √
174 «	213 ╒	252 η
175 »	214 ╓	253 ²
176 ▒	215 ╫	254 ■
177 ▓	216 ╪	255
178 █	217 ┘	
179 │	218 ┌	
180 ┤	219 █	
181 ╡	220 ▄	
182 ╢	221 ▌	
183 ╖	222 ▐	
184 ╕	223 ▀	
185 ╣	224 α	
186 ║	225 β	
187 ╗	226 Γ	
188 ╝	227 π	
189 ╜	228 Σ	
190 ╛	229 σ	
191 ┐	230 μ	
192 └	231 Υ	
193 ┴	232 Φ	
194 ┬	233 Θ	
195 ├	234 Ω	
196 -	235 δ	
197 +	236 ω	
198 ╞	237 φ	
199 ╟	238 ∈	

As you can see, these characters do not appear on your keyboard. But you can enter any of them by holding down the Alt key and typing the numeric value on the numeric keypad (not the regular keyboard). So, to type a lowercase alpha (α), for example, you press Alt and type **224** on the numeric keypad.

The symbols from 176 through 218 are graphics characters, meant for creating boxes, charts, and so on. You can draw single-line figures, double-line figures, and mixed figures, as shown in figure 2.1.

```
C:\>A:FIG2-1

C:\>
```

Figure 2.1. *A double-outline, single-interior line figure drawn using extended characters on the DOS command prompt screen.*

Using ANSI.SYS Functions

Note: Look up ANSI.SYS in DOS's on-screen Help system to see a complete list of commands and codes you can use with ANSI.SYS.

The ANSI.SYS driver provides a wide variety of functions to dress up the command prompt screen, control the location of the cursor, and enhance the functionality of the keyboard. Many older DOS applications depend on ANSI.SYS for screen and keyboard management. But even if your applications don't require it, you can install and use ANSI.SYS yourself. To install ANSI.SYS, insert the following command in CONFIG.SYS:

```
DEVICE=C:\DOS\ANSI.SYS
```

Entering ANSI.SYS Commands

After ANSI.SYS is installed, it scans all standard output, looking
for its own commands. An ANSI.SYS command starts with an
escape character (ASCII 27) followed by a left square bracket ([).
Then one or more numbers follow that select various ANSI.SYS
options. The command must be terminated by a single letter
that identifies the desired function. In other words, an
ANSI.SYS command has this general format:

`ESC[nx`

ESC stands for the escape character, which has no printable
symbol. The *n* stands for the numeric codes; if more than one
code is used, they are separated by semicolons, as in 5;27;16.
The *x* stands for the single-letter code that terminates the
command. The case of the letter is important; commands ending
in capital H, for example, position the cursor, whereas commands
ending in lowercase h set the screen mode. The following
command places the cursor in column 5 of line 12:

`ESC[12;5H`

The following command sets the foreground color to cyan:

`ESC[36m`

When you are typing an ANSI.SYS command, you cannot just
type the letters **E**, **S**, and **C**, as shown in these examples. You
cannot press the Esc key because that causes DOS to clear the
command line; so does holding down Alt and typing the number
27. You have to come up with other ways to send ANSI.SYS
commands to standard output. The three most common ways
are the PROMPT command, a batch file, and a text file.

The PROMPT command substitutes an escape character for the
code $E. The following command sets the foreground color to
cyan, and then issues the normal command prompt:

`PROMPT $E[36m$P$G`

When you enter the command, ANSI.SYS recognizes and
processes the character string `$E[36m`; DOS handles the rest of
the command (`PROMPT $P$G`).

You can include an escape character in a batch file or a text file if
you have an editor that enables you to type an escape character
without interpreting it on the spot. DOS 6's EDIT uses
WordStar's method of inserting special characters into a file:

press Ctrl+P followed by the character you want to insert. In this case, you would press Ctrl+P followed by the Esc key. The escape character appears as a left arrow (←) on-screen. This chapter uses that symbol to represent the escape character in batch and text files.

To execute an ANSI.SYS command from a batch file, place it in an ECHO command. ECHO sends its associated message to standard output where ANSI.SYS will intercept and interpret it. The following batch command sets the foreground text to cyan:

```
ECHO  ←[36m
```

If you include such a command in AUTOEXEC.BAT, you set the initial text color for the command prompt screen during booting. Or you can place the command in its own batch file and execute it separately.

Alternatively, you can place the ANSI.SYS command in a text file and use the TYPE command to display the file. You may create a file called SETCOLOR.TXT that contains just this line:

```
←[36m
```

The command TYPE SETCOLOR.TXT sends the contents of the file to standard output, where ANSI.SYS intercepts and interprets it.

Which method is the best way to execute an ANSI.SYS command? That depends on what you are trying to do. When you want to add some bells and whistles to the output of a batch program, the batch method makes the most sense. To set permanent screen and keyboard characteristics, such as new key definitions and screen colors, a text file works best. The PROMPT command is the best choice for commands that must be repeated constantly. If you want to place the command prompt in a particular position on-screen, for example, you would include the ANSI.SYS command in the PROMPT command.

Dressing Up the Command Prompt, Part 2

You have already seen how to use the PROMPT command to set the foreground color to cyan, but you can get a lot fancier than that. You can display the date, time, and DOS version number

at the top of the screen in red; the command prompt in the
middle of the screen in cyan; and the user's input and command
output in white. You are limited only by the number of characters you can squeeze into the PROMPT command; DOS limits
all commands to 127 characters.

You should keep two DOS characteristics in mind when creating
a fancy PROMPT command. First, DOS stores the command
and rereads it every time it wants to display a command prompt.
So any ANSI.SYS commands buried in there are executed time
the command prompt is displayed. If you move the cursor to line
10 before displaying the command prompt, for example, each
command prompt from then on is displayed on line 10. Second,
DOS and ANSI.SYS process the PROMPT command from left
to right, so you can position the cursor, set a color, display some
text, move the cursor, set another color, display some more text,
and so on.

Suppose that you want to create the command prompt screen
shown in figure 2.2.

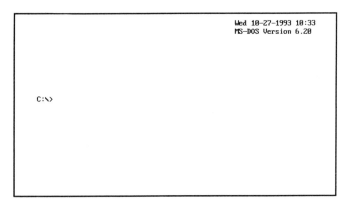

Figure 2.2.   *The command prompt screen as adapted by
ANSI.SYS commands to display the time, date, and version number
and position the cursor on line 10.*

The date, time, and DOS version are displayed in the upper
right corner. The usual command prompt then is displayed on
line 10. (The date and time are refreshed only when the command prompt is redisplayed; if you don't enter any commands
for 10 minutes, the displayed time does not change.) The
following command sets up this screen:

```
PROMPT $E[1;50H$D $T$H$H$H$H$H$H$
➥E[2;50H$V$E[10;1H$P$G
```

The ANSI.SYS command $E[1;50H places the cursor in column 50 of line 1. The PROMPT codes $D THHHHH$H display the date, a space, and the time, backspacing six characters to remove the seconds and hundredths of seconds. Then the ANSI.SYS command $E[2;50H moves the cursor down a line. The PROMPT code $V displays the DOS version number. The ANSI.SYS command $E[10;1H moves the cursor to the first column of line 10. Finally, the PROMPT codes PG display the normal command prompt.

Why not add some color to this screen? In the following command, the ANSI.SYS command $E[31m calls for red foreground text for the date, time, and version number. The command $E[36m requests cyan foreground text for the prompt itself, and $E[37m resets the foreground to white so that the user's input and command output are typed in white. (In the following command, bold type indicates changes from the previous example.)

```
PROMPT $E[1;50H$E[31m$D  $T$H$H$H$H$H$H$E[2;50H$V
➡$E[10;1H$E[36m$P$G$E[37m
```

So far, so good. But displaying the command prompt in the same position every time causes problems. DOS normally displays the command prompt on a blank line, scrolling the screen as necessary to make room. The output from the command follows it, also on blank lines. But when you take over control of the cursor position, DOS no longer seeks out blank lines. The new prompt, your command, and its output are mixed right in with whatever is already on-screen from past commands. The result is utter confusion.

You may think that starting the PROMPT command with $E[2J, which clears the screen, could solve the problem. But when each new command prompt clears the screen, you don't have time to read the output from the preceding command before it disappears. You will not be able to read the reports from commands such as DIR and TREE. It is hard to think of a situation in which $E[2J would be appropriate in a PROMPT command.

The solution to this problem lies in the command $E[s, which saves the current cursor position, along with $E[u, which restores the cursor to the saved position. If you save the current cursor position at the beginning of the PROMPT command, before moving the cursor to line 1, and then restore it just before displaying the normal command prompt, everything works out fine. Figure 2.3 shows the result of the following command; the figure includes some command interactions so that you can see that the next command prompt follows the output from the preceding command:

```
PROMPT $E[s$E[1;50H$E[31m$D
➥ $T$H$H$H$H$H$H$E[2;50H$V$E[u$E[36m$P$G$E[37m
```

```
                                      Wed 10-27-1993 10:31
  C:\>date                            MS-DOS Version 6.20
  Current date is Wed 10-27-1993
  Enter new date (mm-dd-yy):

  C:\>time
  Current time is 10:31:00.52a
  Enter new time:

  C:\>
```

Figure 2.3.   *The command prompt in this example displays the date, time, and DOS version number in the upper right corner in red; the command prompt on the next available line in cyan; and the user's input and command output in white.*

Redefining Keys

An ANSI.SYS command in the form ESC[`"key"` ; `"value"`p defines a value for a key. Place both the key and the new value in quotation marks. The following command assigns the value Æ to the ~ key. The value Æ is typed by pressing Alt+145:

←[`"~"` ; `"Æ"` p

You also can type this command by using the numeric value in place of `"Æ"`; in that case, don't enclose it in quotation marks:

←[`"~"` ;145p

You even can assign an entire string of characters and numeric values to a key. The following command sets up the ~ key to type the expression CD \ followed by a carriage return. In other words, the ~ key becomes a macro that returns the current drive to its root directory:

←[`"~"` ; `"CD \"` ;13p

Remember that values in ANSI.SYS commands must be separated by semicolons. The exception is when you have a string of ASCII characters; instead of typing **"C"**; **"D"**; and so on, you can enclose the entire string in one set of quotation marks. You can mix quoted values with numeric values. In the previous example, the only way to add a carriage return to the end of the value is to type a semicolon followed by the number 13.

Assigning Values to Non-Character Keys

In the previous example, pressing the ~ key would no longer type a ~ character. You probably don't want to reassign too many of your character keys because you need them for their usual functions. But there are many unused non-character keys and key combinations, such as F11 or Ctrl+Shift+A, that have no standard meaning in DOS. All these keys are free for reassignment. You can set up the function keys from Shift+F1 to Alt+F12 to type 36 of the extended characters, for example.

When you want to assign a value to a non-character key or key combination, you have to use a special code to identify the key. The DOS on-screen Help discussion for ANSI.SYS documents the available codes. The code for the Shift+F1 combination, for example, is 0;84. The following command assigns the string DIR followed by a carriage return to Shift+F1, which is represented by the code 0;84:

```
←[0;84;"DIR";13p
```

Reassigning these keys affects the DOS command prompt screen only. The assignments don't even carry into EDIT or DOSSHELL. So don't worry about interfering with functions assigned to the same key combinations in your applications.

Separating the Duplicate Keys

An enhanced keyboard has several duplicate keys. For example, there is a + key on the regular keyboard and another on the numeric keypad. There is a right-arrow key on the numeric keypad and another in the separate arrow-key section. Ordinarily, DOS treats these keys as the same, but you can assign separate functions to them. You use the /X switch on the DEVICE=ANSI.SYS in CONFIG.SYS command to separate the duplicate keys. Then you can assign different functions to them.

Note: Some programs were designed for older keyboards and don't work well with the duplicate keys (the gray ones). You can make an enhanced keyboard appear like a standard keyboard with the command SWITCHES /K in CONFIG.SYS. In that case, the /X switch on ANSI.SYS has no effect and you cannot assign separate functions to the duplicate keys.

3

Batch Programs

When you work at the command prompt, batch programs can make your tasks more powerful. This chapter shows you several techniques you may not have seen before.

Automating Command Execution

Sometimes you don't want to be bothered with keyboard input during a batch job. Commands such as DATE, TIME, DEL *.*, and LABEL require simple input that easily could be bypassed.

Automating Single-Response Commands

Certain commands require a one-letter or one-word response from the user to complete their function. The DATE command, for example, generates a message like this:

```
Current date is Thu 05-10-1993
Enter new date (mm-dd-yy):
```

If you don't want to change the date, you have to press Enter to complete the program. The TIME program behaves similarly. The following command displays today's date without asking for a new one:

```
ECHO. | DATE | FIND "Current"
```

First, it generates a carriage return (the result of ECHO.) and pipes that to the DATE command. Because a carriage return is piped to it, DATE does not wait for a response from the keyboard. It terminates itself without changing the date. And because the standard output from the DATE command is piped

to the FIND command, the full message is never displayed. The
FIND command displays only the line that says `Current date`
`is Thu 05-10-1993`.

> **Note:** The FIND command is case sensitive by
> default, so you must be sure to search for *Current*—
> not *CURRENT* or *current*. Or, you can add /I to
> the FIND command to ignore case.

You can use the same technique to display the current time
without changing it:

```
ECHO. ¦ TIME ¦ FIND "Current"
```

If you prefer to use DEL *.* instead of DELTREE you can
bypass the `Are you sure` question in this way:

```
ECHO Y ¦ DEL *.* > NUL
```

The ECHO command pipes a Y to the DEL command, so DEL
doesn't wait for a keyboard response to `Are you sure`. Because
DEL's output is redirected to NUL, the message never appears
on the monitor.

Automating Multiple-Response Commands

Some commands that you may want to automate cannot be
completed with just a single keyboard input. The FORMAT
command, for example, requires at least two carriage returns plus
an N at the end in response to `Format another (Y/N)?`. Unless
you include a volume label in the command, it also requires a
response to a request for a volume label. As another example, the
LABEL command requires a carriage return and a Y to delete the
current label of a disk. You cannot automate such commands
with ECHO because ECHO can provide only one message.
Instead, you have to place the necessary responses in a file and
redirect the command's standard input to the file. The program
reads one line from the file each time it wants standard input.
Suppose that you want to delete drive B's volume label as part of
a batch program. You could do it with the following commands:

```
1    ECHO. > TEMPIN
2    ECHO Y >> TEMPIN
3    LABEL B: < TEMPIN
4    DEL TEMPIN
```

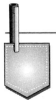

Note: In this and future examples, the commands are numbered for reference purposes only; they would not work if the numbers actually appeared in the batch file.

Command 1 creates (or replaces) a file called TEMPIN and stores a carriage return in it. Command 2 adds a second line containing a Y to the file. Then, command 3 uses TEMPIN as standard input. When it asks `Volume label (11 characters, ENTER for none)?`, it reads the carriage return from TEMPIN. When it asks `Delete current volume label (Y/N)?`, it reads the Y from TEMPIN. The effect is to delete the label of the disk in drive B. Finally, command 4 deletes the temporary file.

Linking to Other Batch Programs

A batch program easily can invoke a nonbatch program, such as an internal or external command, but problems can arise when one batch program tries to invoke another batch program. It can be done, but you have to know what you are doing.

Chaining to a Batch Program

When one batch program executes another batch program without the CALL command, DOS switches to the second batch program and never returns to the first one; this technique is called *chaining*. Suppose that DT.BAT displays the current date and time and you execute it from AUTOEXEC.BAT like this:

```
CLS
ECHO Good Morning!
ECHO.
DT
ECHO.
MEM /P
```

The problem is, after executing the DT command, DOS would never return to AUTOEXEC.BAT for the remaining commands. The final ECHO and MEM commands would never be executed.

In general, avoid chaining except from the final command in a batch file, where it does no harm. You occasionally may find it a handy way to exit early from a batch program when a certain condition turns out to be true. You will see more about handling conditions later in this chapter.

Calling another Batch Program

When you use the CALL command to link to another batch program (a *called program*), DOS returns to the first program (the *calling program*) when the called program terminates. It resumes execution with the line following the CALL command. The following set of commands executes DT.BAT, and then continues with other processing. The only difference between these lines and the earlier example is the word CALL and a path inserted in front of the DT command:

```
CLS
ECHO Good Morning!
ECHO.
CALL C:\BATCHES\DT
ECHO.
MEM /P
```

Tip: Always specify the path when you reference another batch program. It saves DOS time in finding the program.

In all your batch programs, be sure to use CALL in front of any command that invokes another batch program unless you intentionally want to chain to the second batch.

Calling Batch Programs from DOSKEY Macros

DOSKEY macros also can invoke batch programs, and, just like a batch file, they must use the CALL command to avoid terminating the macro early. The following macro definition calls the DT program to display the date and time:

```
DOSKEY RESET=C: $T CD C:\ $T CALL C:\BATCHES\DT
➡ $T PAUSE $T CLS
```

Using the Numeric Variables

You can use up to 10 numeric variables, %0 through %9, in a batch file. DOS replaces them with information from the command line when you execute the batch program. The following command shows how DOS assigns the numeric variables to the parts of a command:

```
%0     %1     %2     %3
MDEL *.BAK *.TMP *.OLD
```

As you can see, %0 always refers to the command name; you will not find much use for it. %1 refers to the first parameter, %2 to the second parameter, and so on up to the ninth parameter. These parameters help to make a program more flexible by supplying specific information, such as filespecs, at execution time.

The following batch program, VAULT.BAT, backs files from the hard drive to the drive specified as the first parameter. First, VAULT.BAT formats the floppy, using the second parameter as the volume label (commands 2 through 9). Then it moves the files specified by the third parameter to the floppy (commands 10 and 11). The filespec can be specific or global.

```
1    @ECHO OFF
2    ECHO Place the target disk in drive %1

3    REM Prepare temporary input file for FORMAT
     ➥command
4    ECHO. > TEMPIN
5    ECHO N >> TEMPIN

6    REM Format target disk
7    FORMAT %1 /V:%2 < TEMPIN > NUL

8    REM Delete temporary input file
9    DEL TEMPIN

10   REM Move file(s) to the target disk
11   MOVE %3 %1
```

As you can see from this example, you can use a numeric variable more than once, and you don't have to use them in order, although you cannot skip one.

Suppose that you want to use VAULT.BAT to move all your WK* files from C:\93BUDGET to drive B. You would enter the following command:

```
VAULT B: BUDGETVAULT C:\93BUDGET\*.WK*
```

After DOS replaces the numeric variables, the VAULT program looks like this:

```
@ECHO OFF
ECHO Place the target disk in drive B:

REM Prepare temporary input file for FORMAT command
ECHO. > TEMPIN
ECHO N >> TEMPIN

REM Format target disk
FORMAT B: /V:BUDGETVAULT < TEMPIN > NUL

REM Delete temporary input file
DEL TEMPIN

REM Move files to the target disk
MOVE C:\93BUDGET\*.WK* B:
```

Planning for Improper Parameters

When you decide what numeric variables to use where, keep in mind what will happen if the user enters improper or null values. In the previous example, if someone enters VAULT with no parameters, DOS will try, and fail, to process the following FORMAT command:

```
FORMAT /V < TEMPIN > NUL
```

This command fails for two reasons: it specifies no drive name, and the /V: parameter is invalid. After the FORMAT command fails, the DEL command removes the temporary file. Then, the MOVE command fails because it has no parameters. In this situation, the FORMAT and MOVE commands should fail, so all is well.

Note: You can test for omitted parameters with the IF command. See "Making Decisions Based on Variables," later in this chapter.

Be sure to analyze your batch programs to make sure that nothing disastrous happens if someone omits a parameter or enters an invalid parameter.

Using Environment Variables

Note: Chapter 12 explains the DOS environment and how to set environment variables.

Another way to provide variables in a batch program is to use environment variables. A variable stored in the environment lasts until you reboot, exit the current environment, or change or delete the variable. So once a variable has been set, you can access it from several programs.

Only programs and batch programs can access variables in the environment. You cannot use them at the command prompt or in DOSKEY macros. To use an environment variable in a batch program, enclose its name in percent signs (%). Suppose that the environment contains the following variable:

```
USERID=North
```

You could include the following command in a batch program:

```
ECHO Hello, %USERID%
```

At execution time, DOS substitutes NORTH for %USERID%, resulting in the following message:

```
Hello, North
```

Appending an Environment Variable

You can append a value to the beginning or end of an existing
environment variable. The PATH variable provides a good
example. Suppose that you want to insert C:\TEMPDIR to the
beginning of the path. You could do it like this:

```
SET PATH=C: \TEMPDIR; %PATH%
```

This command sets the PATH variable, using its own current
value—whatever that is—as part of the new value. The
%PATH% expression causes DOS to insert the current
path (if any) into the command.

Saving and Restoring the Current Value

If you want to change the variable only temporarily—say until
the batch program ends—you can add commands to save and
restore the original variable:

```
REM Save the current path
SET OLDPATH=%PATH%

REM Insert TEMPDIR in the path
SET PATH=C:\TEMPDIR;%PATH%

[the rest of the program]

REM Restore the original path
SET PATH=%OLDPATH%

REM Eliminate OLDPATH
SET OLDPATH=
```

Note: You can use this technique to temporarily
move a directory to the beginning of the search
path to cut access times for the program referenced
in a batch job. No harm is done if a directory
appears twice in the search path.

Branching

DOS includes IF and GOTO commands so that you can decide
what to do next in a batch program based on current conditions.
Thus, you can create multiple execution paths, or branches, in
your program. Unfortunately, you can test only a few conditions,
as you will see in the following sections.

Making Decisions Based on File Presence

> **Note:** Look up IF in DOS's on-screen Help system
> to see its syntax, notes, and examples.

A command in the form IF EXIST *filespec command* tests for the
presence of at least one file that matches *filespec.* If a file is found,
DOS executes the specified *command.* In the following example,
if AUTOEXEC.BAT exists in the root directory of drive C, it is
renamed as AUTOEXEC.SAV:

```
IF EXIST C:\AUTOEXEC.BAT REN C:\AUTOEXEC.BAT
➡AUTOEXEC.SAV
```

IF EXIST helps to prevent command failure when a file does
not exist. The REN command, if used by itself, generates an
error message that may confuse an inexperienced user when
C:\AUTOEXEC.BAT is not found. IF EXIST suppresses the
REN command when AUTOEXEC.BAT is not present.

> **Warning:** IF EXIST senses hidden and system files,
> whereas a command like REN does not, so you could
> still run into situations in which the condition turns
> out to be positive but the enclosed command fails.

Testing for a Directory

IF EXIST will not recognize a directory, but you can test for the
NUL file name, which is implied in every directory. The
following command sets the TEMP variable only if the
C:\TEMPDIR directory exists:

```
IF EXIST C:\TEMPDIR\NUL SET TEMP=C:\TEMPDIR
```

Negating the Condition

IF NOT EXIST does the opposite of IF EXIST. DOS executes
the enclosed command only if it finds no file that matches the
filespec. In versions of DOS before 6.2, it helps to prevent
overwriting an existing file with a MOVE, COPY, or XCOPY
command. The following command copies AUTOEXEC.BAT
from A:\ to C:\ only if it does not exist on C:

```
IF NON EXIST C:\AUTOEXEC.BAT
➥ COPY A:\AUTOEXEC.BAT C:\
```

Note: In DOS 6.2, the commands XCOPY,
COPY, and MOVE warn you before overwriting
files. Chapter 7 explains more about this new
feature.

Making Decisions Based on Variables

A command in the format IF *string1*==*string2 command* causes
the specified *command* to be executed only if the two parameters
specified by *string1* and *string2* are identical. This command
enables you test the value of a numeric or environment variable.
The following command, for example, displays the message Done
only if the %1 parameter is /C:

```
IF "%1"=="/C" ECHO Done
```

Note: Yes, you have to use two equal signs.

Suppose that you are designing a batch program to move files to the disk in drive A. The %1 parameter specifies the name of the files to be moved. You want to offer the option of formatting the disk first. You can set up your program so that the disk is formatted only if a user includes /F as the %2 parameter.

The following command tests to see whether the second parameter on the invoking command is an /F; if so, it formats the disk:

```
IF "%2"=="/F" FORMAT B: < TEMPIN > NUL
```

Suppose that the second parameter is /F. When /F replaces %2, DOS receives the following command. The condition is TRUE and the FORMAT command is executed:

```
IF "/F"=="/F" FORMAT B: < TEMPIN > NUL
```

Suppose that the second parameter is /B instead of /F. DOS receives the following command; the condition is FALSE and the FORMAT command is not executed:

```
IF "/B"=="/F" FORMAT B: < TEMPIN > NUL
```

DOS receives the following command if the second parameter has been omitted. Again, the condition is FALSE and the disk is not formatted:

```
IF ""=="/F" FORMAT B: < TEMPIN > NUL
```

This example demonstrates why you need to place quotation marks around *string1* and *string2* in most cases. DOS sees "" as a valid *string1* with a null value. Without the quotation marks, DOS receives the following command, which causes a syntax error because there is no *string1*:

```
IF ==/F FORMAT B: < TEMPIN > NUL
```

Use quotation marks around both strings in any case where either string may be null after parameter substitution.

You also can test environment variables with IF *string1==string2*. The following command sets the TEMP variable only if one does not currently exist:

```
IF "%TEMP%"=="" SET TEMP=C:\TEMPDIR
```

Tip: You can use the IF command in DOSKEY macros and at the command prompt, although you cannot reference environment variables in those two settings.

Making Decisions Based on the Exit Code

Many programs set an exit code when they terminate. The exit code is a number between 0 and 255 indicating whether the program succeeded or failed and, if it failed, what went wrong. FIND, for example, sets the following exit codes:

Code	Meaning
0	At least one match was found.
1	No matches were found but no errors were encountered.
2	Some kind of error was encountered; for example, the specified input file could not be opened.

Exit codes are not standardized. You must look through a program's documentation to find the meanings of its exit codes. DOS 6's on-screen Help system documents the exit codes for those DOS utilities that set them. In most cases, exit code 0 indicates success.

When you execute a program from a batch job, you can test the exit code immediately afterward using the command IF ERRORLEVEL *n* command. DOS executes the specified command only if the current exit code is equal to or greater than the specified ERRORLEVEL value. The following command, for example, displays a message if the preceding program failed for any reason:

```
IF ERRORLEVEL 1 ECHO Sorry. Try again later.
```

If the preceding program set an exit code of 0, the condition is FALSE (0 is not equal to or greater than 1) and the message is not displayed. If the preceding program set any other exit code, the condition is TRUE and the message is displayed.

Calling Another Program to Process a True Condition

IF permits only one command to be specified for a TRUE condition. But you often cannot handle a TRUE condition with only one command. Take the following command shown below, which you saw earlier:

```
IF "%2"=="/F" FORMAT B: < TEMPIN > NUL
```

You may want to include commands to create and delete the TEMPIN file as well as to warn the user that the disk will be reformatted. But how can you do that when only one command can be included in the IF command?

One solution is to call another batch program that processes the TRUE condition. You can create a FORMB.BAT file that contains these commands:

```
@ECHO OFF
ECHO Place the target disk in drive B.
ECHO Warning! Any existing data on this disk
➥ will be destroyed.
PAUSE
ECHO. > TEMPIN
ECHO. >> TEMPIN
ECHO N >> TEMPIN
FORMAT B: < TEMPIN > NUL
DEL TEMPIN
```

Now you can call FORMB.BAT from your IF command:

```
IF "%2"=="/F" CALL C:\BATCHES\FORMB
```

Using GOTO to Create a Separate Branch to Handle a Condition

Note: Look up GOTO in DOS's on-line Help system to see its syntax, notes, and examples.

Another way to provide several commands to handle a condition uses the GOTO command to branch to another part of the same program. This solution has the advantage of keeping all the processing within one program; it takes DOS less time to find the code, and it places fewer files on your hard disk.

To solve the problem with GOTO, set up the IF command to jump to the next section if %2 is not /F. If it is /F, the commands immediately following the IF command are executed. You can use as many commands as necessary to process the /F parameter. The entire routine looks something like this:

```
IF NOT "%2"=="/F" GOTO NEXTPART
REM The following commands are processed only if
➡%2 = /F
ECHO Place the target disk in drive B.
ECHO Warning! Any existing data on this disk
➡will be destroyed.
PAUSE
ECHO. > TEMPIN
ECHO N >> TEMPIN
FORMAT B: < TEMPIN > NUL
DEL TEMPIN

:NEXTPART
REM The following commands are processed whether
➡or not %2 = /F
```

Look at another example using a GOTO branch. Earlier, you saw how this command sets the TEMP variable if it does not already exist:

```
IF "%TEMP%"=="" SET TEMP=C:\TEMPDIR
```

Suppose that C:\TEMPDIR does not yet exist and you need to create it as part of the routine. You can do it like this:

```
IF NOT "%TEMP%"=="" GOTO NEXTSTEP
REM The next two commands are executed only if
➡TEMP doesn't exist
MD C:\TEMPDIR
SET TEMP=C:\TEMPDIR

:NEXTSTEP
REM The program continues on from here.
```

Processing Multiple Exit Codes

When you are processing an exit code, you often need to write routines for more than one of the possible codes. After a FIND command, for example, you may want to display the following messages:

Exit Code	Meaning	Message
0	At least one string was found	FIND was successful
1	No string was found but no error was encountered	The %1 file was searched but the %2 string was not found
2	An error occurred	FIND could not open the %1 file; make sure the filespec is correct and try again

You need several IF commands to accomplish this. The task is complicated by the fact that IF ERRORLEVEL is TRUE if the exit code is equal to or greater than the specified value. Suppose that you just supply the following commands:

```
IF ERRORLEVEL 0 ECHO FIND was successful
IF ERRORLEVEL 1 ECHO The %1 file was searched
➡but the %2 string was not found.
IF ERRORLEVEL 2 ECHO FIND could not open the
➡%1 file; correct the filespec and try again.
```

These commands work well when the exit code is 0; only the first condition is TRUE and only the first message is displayed. But when the exit code is 1, IF ERRORLEVEL 0 and IF ERRORLEVEL 1 are TRUE and both messages are displayed. Similarly, when the exit code is 2, all three messages are displayed.

To avoid displaying multiple messages, you have to use GOTO to branch around subsequent IF commands after you have identified the correct exit code. And you have to work from the top down so that IF ERRORLEVEL 0 does not turn out to be TRUE for all exit codes. The correct routine looks like this:

```
IF ERRORLEVEL 2 GOTO ERROR
IF ERRORLEVEL 1 GOTO NOTFOUND

REM If DOS reaches this line, the exit code is 0.
ECHO FIND was successful.
GOTO ENDING

:NOT FOUND
ECHO The %1 file was searched but the %2 string
➥was not found.
GOTO ENDING

:ERROR
ECHO FIND could not open the %1 file;
➥correct the filespec and try again.

:ENDING
REM The program continues from here.
```

These lines stand as a model for any routine that processes
multiple branches. Keep the following points in mind when
designing your own multiple branches:

- Be sure to process exit codes from the top down.

- You don't have to write an IF command for the lowest exit
  code; DOS reaches the lines that follow the last IF
  command automatically if none of the earlier IF commands turn out to be TRUE.

- You don't have to write a separate IF command for every
  exit code the program can issue. If you want to handle
  codes 12 and above with one routine, codes 2 through 10
  with another routine, and codes 0 and 1 with a third
  routine, you need only two IF commands:

  IF ERRORLEVEL 12... (captures exit codes above 12)
  IF ERRORLEVEL 2... (captures exit codes between 2 and
  ➥12)

- Two or more IF commands can branch to the same label if
  their conditions are to be handled in the same manner.

- Be sure that each routine that handles an exit code ends
  with a GOTO command to branch past the next routines,
  so that only one routine is executed. The final routine does
  not need a GOTO command.

Using IF with IF

The command contained in an IF command can itself be an IF command. The following command, for example, calls the program named C:\SETBOOT.BAT only if C:\COMMAND. COM and C:\AUTOEXEC.BAT do not exist:

```
IF NOT EXIST C:\COMMAND.COM IF NOT EXIST
➥C:\AUTOEXEC.BAT CALL C:\SETBOOT
```

The first condition is IF NOT EXIST C:\COMMAND.COM. Only if it is TRUE—that is, only if C:\COMMAND.COM is missing—is the second IF command processed. So both conditions have to be TRUE for the CALL C:\SETBOOT command to be processed.

The two conditions in this example have what is known as an AND relationship. That is, both condition A and condition B must be true for the final command to be processed. Any time you want to test for an AND relationship, nest the second IF command inside the first IF command as shown here. In fact, you can include several levels of nesting if need be. The following command calls C:\BATCHES\BADKEY.BAT if %1 is not Y, y, N, or n:

```
IF NOT "%1"=="Y" IF NOT "%1"=="y" IF NOT "%1"=="N"
➥IF NOT "%1"=="n" CALL C:\BATCHES\BADKEY
```

Establishing OR Relationships

Suppose that you want to establish an OR relationship between two conditions. You may want to branch to the routine labeled FLOPPY if %1 is either A or B, for example. You do that by placing separate IF commands—one after the other:

```
IF "%1"=="A" GOTO FLOPPY
IF "%1"=="B" GOTO FLOPPY
```

Suppose that you want to call SETBOOT if COMMAND.COM or AUTOEXEC.BAT is missing. You may want to try the following two commands:

```
IF NOT EXIST C:\COMMAND.COM CALL C:\BATCHES\SETBOOT
IF NOT EXIST C:\AUTOEXEC.BAT CALL C:\BATCHES\SETBOOT
```

As shown, these commands call SETBOOT twice if both COMMAND.COM and AUTOEXEC.BAT are missing. If that is not desirable, you can adapt the second command to call

SETBOOT only if AUTOEXEC.BAT is missing and
COMMAND.COM is present:

```
IF NOT EXIST C:\COMMAND.COM CALL C:\BATCHES\SETBOOT
IF NOT EXIST C:\AUTOEXEC.BAT IF EXIST C:\COMMAND.COM
➥CALL C:\BATCHES\SETBOOT
```

Using Nested IFs with Multiple Exit Codes

Another way to handle multiple exit codes is to use nested IFs to
make sure that the exit code is a specific number. The following
command, for example, branches to EXIT4 if the exit code is
equal to or greater than 4 but is not equal to or greater than 5; in
other words, if it is exactly 4:

```
IF ERRORLEVEL 4 IF NOT ERRORLEVEL 5 GOTO EXIT4
```

The following routine uses nested IFs to accomplish the same
exit-code processing that you saw before. Because this routine
pins down the exact exit codes, they don't have to be processed
in reverse order: ·

```
IF ERRORLEVEL 0 IF NOT ERRORLEVEL 1 GOTO EXIT0
IF ERRORLEVEL 1 IF NOT ERRORLEVEL 2 GOTO EXIT1
IF ERRORLEVEL 2 GOTO EXIT2

:EXIT0
ECHO FIND was successful.
GOTO ENDING

:EXIT1
ECHO The %1 file was searched but the %2 string
➥was not found.
GOTO ENDING

:EXIT2
ECHO FIND could not open the %1 file; correct the
➥filespec and try again.
:ENDING
REM The program continues from here.
```

Some people prefer this method because they think the overall
structure of the routine is clearer when it goes from 0 up. Others

prefer the first method because they think the unnested IFs are clearer than the nested IFs.

Some notes about this second routine:

■ You could omit the line beginning with `IF ERRORLEVEL 2` and place the commands to handle exit code 2 immediately after the IF commands, but the structure is clearer this way.

■ To handle a range of codes from *m* through *n* with one routine, use `IF ERRORLEVEL m IF NOT ERRORLEVEL` *n*+1. For example, the condition `IF ERRORLEVEL 4 IF NOT ERRORLEVEL 8` captures exit codes 4 through 7.

Using Variables as Labels

You can use a variable name as the target of a GOTO statement. As always, DOS replaces the variable with the actual value at execution time, determining which routine is actually executed. Suppose that your computer is shared by three people and the current user's name is contained in the environment variable USERID. AUTOEXEC.BAT may contain the following routine to personalize the configuration for the individual user:

```
GOTO %USERID%

:JUDI
REM The following commands set up the correct
➥configuration for Judi
...
GOTO ENDING

:GREG
REM The following commands set up the correct
➥configuration for Donna
...
GOTO ENDING

:KARLA
REM The following commands set up the correct
➥configuration for Karla
...

:ENDING
```

```
REM No matter which user branch was executed,
➡processing continues here.
```

You can use this same technique to process exit codes. The following routine sets an environment variable named JUMPER to EXIT0, EXIT1, or EXIT2, and then branches to the value of JUMPER. At the end, it deletes JUMPER from the environment. (The routines represented by EXIT0, EXIT1, and EXIT2 are the same as those you have seen before:)

```
IF ERRORLEVEL 0 IF ERRORLEVEL NOT 1 SET JUMPER=EXIT0
IF ERRORLEVEL 1 IF NOT ERRORLEVEL NOT 2 SET
➡JUMPER=EXIT1
IF ERRORLEVEL 2 SET JUMPER=EXIT2
GOTO %JUMPER%

:EXIT0
...
GOTO ENDING

:EXIT1
...
GOTO ENDING

:EXIT2
...

:ENDING
SET JUMPER=
```

You also can use a numeric variable as the target of a GOTO command. Suppose that %1 can be TAPE or DISK. You can process it like this:

```
GOTO %1

:TAPE
REM The following commands process the TAPE
➡variable.
...
GOTO ENDING

:DISK
```

```
REM The following commands process the DISK
➥variable.
...
```

```
:ENDING
```

> **Note:** In this example, the GOTO %1 command results in an error message if %1 is not TAPE or DISK.

Getting User Input during a Batch Program

> **Note:** Look up CHOICE in DOS's on-line Help system to see its syntax, notes, and examples.

DOS 6 includes a new command that enables you to display a question on the keyboard and read a one-character response from the keyboard. The CHOICE command sets the exit code based on the user's response. The program can then branch according to the exit code.

Suppose that a batch program formats a floppy disk. For safety's sake, it checks the disk for files first. If any files exist, the program warns the user and asks whether it should proceed with the format. The user presses Y or N. As you can see in the following lines, you process CHOICE's exit code just like any other exit code:

```
REM Check for files on the target disk
IF NOT EXIST B:\*.* GOTO FORMSTEP
```

```
REM Ask the user what to do
ECHO The target disk is not empty
CHOICE Would you like to format it anyway
REM Process exit codes from CHOICE
IF ERRORLEVEL 1 IF NOT ERRORLEVEL 2 GOTO FORMSTEP
IF ERRORLEVEL 2 IF NOT ERRORLEVEL 3 GOTO EXIT2
IF ERRORLEVEL 255 GOTO EXIT255

:EXIT2
REM The user pressed N
ECHO Try again with another disk
GOTO ENDING

:EXIT255
REM The user pressed an invalid key
ECHO You pressed an invalid key. Program terminated.
GOTO ENDING

:FORMSTEP
REM Either there are no files on the disk or
➥the user pressed Y
ECHO. > TEMPIN
ECHO. >> TEMPIN
ECHO N >> TEMPIN
FORMAT B: < TEMPIN > NUL
DEL TEMPIN

REM The following steps continue with the program
...

:ENDING
REM The end of the program
```

Figure 3.1 shows what the screen looks like when the CHOICE command is executed. Notice that CHOICE adds the [Y/N]? prompt to the end of the message.

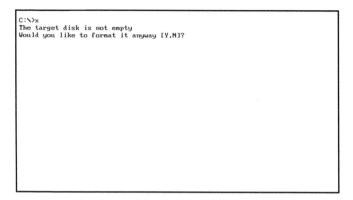

```
C:\>x
The target disk is not empty
Would you like to format it anyway [Y,N]?
```

Figure 3.1.   *The result of a CHOICE command.*

Displaying a Menu

You can use the ECHO and CHOICE commands to create a
menu system like the one shown in figure 3.2. In this case, the
menu is designed to act as the user's main access to the system; it
appears on-screen whenever the user is not using the database,
scheduler, or word processor. You can just as easily design a
menu system that offers choices within the current batch
program only and disappears when the batch job is over.

```
===================================================
                  Main Menu
          D    Database
          S    Scheduler
          W    Word Processor
          X    Exit
===================================================

Your choice:
```

Figure 3.2.   *Using ECHO and CHOICE to create a menu.*

The following commands display and process the main menu shown in the figure:

```
1    @ECHO OFF
2    :SHOWMENU
3    CLS
4    ECHO.
5    ECHO.
6    ECHO==========================================
7    ECHO.
8    ECHO                              Main Menu
9    ECHO.
10   ECHO               D      Data Base
11   ECHO               S      Scheduler
12   ECHO               W      Word Processor
13   ECHO               X      Exit
14   ECHO.
15   ECHO==========================================
16   ECHO.
17   ECHO.
18   CHOICE /C:DSWX /N Your choice:
19   REM Process the exit codes from CHOICE
20   IF ERRORLEVEL 1 IF NOT ERRORLEVEL 2 GOTO D
21   IF ERRORLEVEL 2 IF NOT ERRORLEVEL 3 GOTO S
22   IF ERRORLEVEL 3 IF NOT ERRORLEVEL 4 GOTO W
23   IF ERRORLEVEL 4 IF NOT ERRORLEVEL 5 GOTO ENDING
24   IF ERRORLEVEL 255 GOTO BADKEY

25   :D
26   REM The following commands process choice D
27   ...
28   GOTO SHOWMENU

29   :S
30   REM The following commands process choice S
31   ...
32   GOTO SHOWMENU

33   :W
34   REM The following commands process choice W
35   ...
36   GOTO SHOWMENU
```

```
37   :BADKEY
38   REM The following commands handle an
➡invalid choice
39   ...
40   GOTO SHOWMENU

41   :ENDING
42   CLS
43   REM The end of the program
```

Line 3 clears the screen so that the menu is the only thing showing. Lines 4 through 17 display the menu. (This example does not use ANSI.SYS. The menu could be made much more attractive using the functions described in chapter 2.)

Line 18 displays the message `Your choice:` and reads the user's response. The /D switch establishes D, S, W, and X as the valid input keys; CHOICE numbers them from left to right and sets exit code 1 if D is pressed, exit code 2 if S is pressed, and so on. The /N switch suppresses CHOICE's default prompt of (`D/S/W/X`)? after the message.

Lines 20 through 24 branch to the appropriate routine based on the exit code set by CHOICE. Notice that exit code 4 branches immediately to the end of the program because the user has chosen the Exit option.

Lines 25 through 28 handle choice D (they probably start a database program). Line 29 jumps back to line 2 (:SHOWMENU) so that the menu is displayed again when the database program terminates. When you don't want to keep the menu on the screen all the time, you would branch to the end of the program at this point rather than back to the beginning. Similarly, lines 29 through 32 handle choice S, and lines 33 through 36 handle choice W.

Lines 37 through 40 handle exit code 255, which means that the user pressed an invalid key. They probably display some kind of error message. Then the menu is redisplayed.

Looping

The main menu example introduced a *loop*; the same commands are processed again and again until some event terminates the loop. In the main menu example, the loop is ended when the user chooses X from the menu. Other types of loops may be repeated a certain number of times or until all variable parameters have been processed.

Creating Loops with IF and GOTO

Suppose that you want to write a batch program to move files to the disk in drive B. You can set it up so that any number of filespecs can be processed, up to the 127-character limit for all DOS commands.

The following program accomplishes this task:

```
1    @ECHO OFF
2    :START
3    IF "%1"=="" GOTO ENDING
4    MOVE %1 B:
5    SHIFT
6    GOTO START

7    :ENDING
8    REM The program ends here
```

Lines 2 through 6 comprise the loop. Line 2 provides a label (:START) that marks the start of the loop. Line 3 tests to see whether %1 is null. If it is, there are no more filespecs to be processed and the program branches to ENDING to terminate the loop and the program. Lines 4 through 6 are executed only if %1 is not null.

Line 4 moves the file(s) specified by %1 to drive B. Then line 5 shifts the invoking command's parameters to the left so that the next parameter becomes %1, setting up %1 for the next loop. If the invoking command includes five filespecs, %1 accesses the first parameter the first time the loop is processed, the second parameter for the second loop, the third parameter for the third loop, and so on. At the end of the fifth loop, the SHIFT command causes %1 to become null because there is no sixth parameter. Then the IF command at the beginning of the sixth loop is TRUE, and you branch out of the loop and end the program.

This small program stands as a model for all programs that process an unknown number of variable parameters. In fact, by replacing only line 4, you can adapt the program to delete files, copy files, change file attributes, and so on.

Creating Loops with FOR

Note: Look up FOR in DOS's on-line Help system to see its syntax, notes, and examples.

DOS's FOR command was designed specifically for repetitive processing. It repeats a specified command for each item in a list. The following command resets four drives to their root directories:

```
FOR %D IN (A: B: C: D:) DO CD %D\
```

In this example, the expression FOR %D sets up %D as the name of the replaceable variable that is used in the DO *command* at the end of the line. The expression IN (A: B: C: D:) establishes the item list. The expression DO CD %D\ identifies the command to be repeated. In the first iteration, %D is replaced by A:, creating the command CD A:\. Similarly, the second iteration executes CD B:\, the third CD C:\, and the fourth CD D:\.

This command works at the command prompt but not in a batch file. Because of the way DOS processes percent signs (%) in batches, you have to double them, as follows:

```
FOR %%D IN (A: B: C: D:) DO CD %%D\
```

The item list in a FOR command can contain such items as directories (for a DELTREE command, perhaps), filespecs, or even numbered or environmental variables.

If a global filespec appears in the list, a separate DO command is issued for each file that matches the filespec. This may not be the most efficient way to handle a problem, for example, XCOPY *.BAT B: copies the BAT files as a group, but FOR %F IN (*.BAT) DO XCOPY %F B: issues a separate XCOPY command for each BAT file, which takes much longer.

It is hard to use FOR to process an unknown number of items. You can do it by using an environment variable, but the process is somewhat awkward. The following command inserts the current value of the variable named TEMPLIST in the item list:

```
FOR %%F IN (%TEMPLIST%) DO ATTRIB %%F +H
```

To set the attributes of *.EXE, *.BAT, and *.COM files, you
issue this command before starting the batch program:

```
SET TEMPLIST=*.EXE *.BAT *.COM
```

If this process does not appeal to you, you may create your loop
using IF, GOTO, and SHIFT as shown in "Creating Loops with
IF and GOTO."

Processing Multiple Commands with FOR

As with IF, you can specify only one DO command at the end of
FOR. If you need to process several commands for each item in
the list, you can call a second batch program to handle the job.
The following command calls C:\BATCHES\VAULT.BAT for
each DOC, DOT, FIG, and TAB file in the current directory.
The current filespec is passed to VAULT as a parameter.

```
FOR %%F IN (*.DOC *.DOT *.FIG *.TAB)
➥DO CALL C:\BATCHES\VAULT %%F
```

Unlike IF, you cannot use a GOTO command at the end of
FOR. If you do, you branch away from the FOR command and
it is never repeated.

Designing Batches to Run from Floppy Disks

Floppy-disk-only systems are rare these days, and you may be
safe in assuming that your batch program always will be run
from a hard disk. But if there is a possibility that it will be run
from floppy disk, keep in mind that the user may need a chance
to replace the disk containing the program with a target disk
before continuing. Also note that DOS reads only one batch
command at a time from the disk. If you issue a PAUSE
command to give the user time to change a disk, DOS must ask
for the program disk again to read the next command. So the
PAUSE command is, in essence, useless.

Taking Advantage of DOS's Program Priority

The chart shown in figure 3.3 shows how a command is
processed. In the chart, the command DRAW! is entered from
the console. If any terminate-and-stay-resident programs such as

DOSKEY and ANSI.SYS are loaded, they examine the command first, looking for their own commands. If none of the TSRs decide to process the command, it passes to DOS.

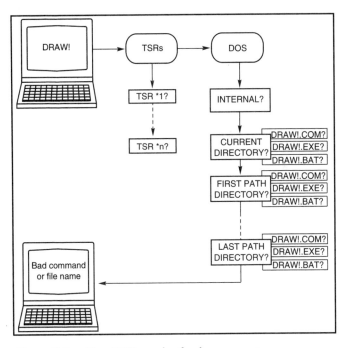

Figure 3.3. *How DOS searches for the program to process a command.*

DOS looks first to see whether it is an internal command. Because DRAW! is not internal, DOS next looks for an external program. It examines the current directory for DRAW!.COM, DRAW!.EXE, and DRAW!.BAT, in that order. (Notice that batch files come last.) If no program file is found in the current directory, DOS begins examining the search path defined in the PATH environment variable. DOS examines each directory in turn, looking first for DRAW!.COM, then for DRAW!.EXE, and finally for DRAW!.BAT. As soon as DOS finds a program file named DRAW!, it loads the program and discontinues the search. Additional program files named DRAW! are not found.

If DOS reaches the end of the search path without finding DRAW!.COM, DRAW!.EXE, or DRAW!.BAT, it displays the message Bad command or file name and waits for the next command.

You can do a couple of things to help DOS find your program files faster:

- Include the path and the extension with the command name. You can do this at the command prompt, as in C:\BATCHES\DRAW!.BAT, and in a batch program, as in CALL C:\BATCHES\DRAW!.BAT. This causes DOS to bypass its normal search pattern and to go immediately to C:\BATCHES to look for DRAW!.BAT. (You can do the same thing with COM and EXE programs to help DOS find commands faster.)

- If you don't want to specify the path and extension every time you access a BAT file, keep all your batch files in one directory, such as C:\BATCHES, and place that directory at the beginning of the search path. (If you do this and give a batch file the same name as a COM or EXE file, as in FORMAT.BAT, DOS will find the batch file, not the COM or EXE file, unless the COM or EXE file is in the current directory. Thus, the batch file overrides the COM or EXE file.)

Using Recursion

A batch program can call itself, creating a loop that executes until something stops it. This technique is known as *recursion*. The following batch program, named LOOPY.BAT, executes until the user presses Ctrl+C or Ctrl+Break to stop it:

```
@ECHO OFF
ECHO Help! I'm being held prisoner in a PC clone.
➡Press Ctrl+C to release me.
CALL LOOPY.BAT
```

Most loops are more easily created by the other techniques in this chapter, but you should be aware that you can use recursion if that will solve a problem you are working on.

DOS Shell

With DOS 6.2, Microsoft dropped DOS Shell on the grounds that most people who want a graphical user interface are using Windows. But if you are working with DOS 5.*x* or 6.0, you still have DOS Shell available to you. And if you upgraded to DOS 6.2 from one of these products, the installation program didn't erase DOS Shell from your DOS directory. If you didn't erase it yourself, it's still there and you can still use it. If you don't have DOS Shell and want it, you can get it from Microsoft. See your DOS 6.2 documentation to find out how.

If you have Windows, don't bother with DOS Shell (or this chapter). Windows is a much better product: But if you're one of those people who cannot use Windows for some reason, DOS Shell is better than no graphical interface at all. This chapter shows you some of the things you can do with the Shell.

What DOS Shell Does

The Shell looks a bit like a "Mickey Mouse" feature to an experienced user, but in reality it is one of DOS's best power tools—as long as you don't have Windows (see fig. 4.1). You can, for example, process in one command files that don't fit into a global filespec—in fact, they can be in different directories. You can move and copy files by dragging them to another drive or directory with your mouse. And you get a chance to confirm all file and directory deletions along with all moves and copies. Finally, you can start up several programs at once, switching between them as needed to accomplish your work.

The Shell offers several powerful ways to launch and run programs: You can start them from the file list, the program list, or the File Run command. The program list enables you to create the graphical interface equivalent of batch programs, but with much more control. You can set up default values for the numeric variables (%1 through %9), including the currently selected file. You can password-protect program groups and individual programs; although the protection is somewhat weak, it will stop an inexperienced user from accessing inappropriate programs. You also can control whether task swapping should be permitted and, if so, what task swapping shortcut keys can and cannot be used.

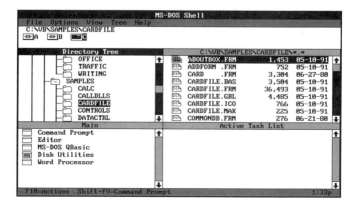

Figure 4.1. *The DOS Shell screen, showing the menu bar, drive list, directory tree, file list, program list, and message/status line.*

You can configure the Shell screen to a certain extent to suit your hardware and your work style. You can pick the best color scheme (or design your own) and choose the best view for the current task. As you will see at the end of this chapter, you can even set up multiple configurations and share your configuration with others in your work group.

Views of the Shell Screen

The Shell offers several views (see fig. 4.2). The default view is called Program/File Lists because it shows file information at the top of the screen and a program list at the bottom. If you don't use the program list, you can eliminate it and give more room to the file information with Single File List. When you want to move or copy files, the Dual File Lists come in handy. And if you want to work exclusively with the program list, you can eliminate the file information by choosing the Program List view.

No one view is perfect all the time. You will find yourself switching views according to what task you want to accomplish. You see several applications of these views later in this chapter.

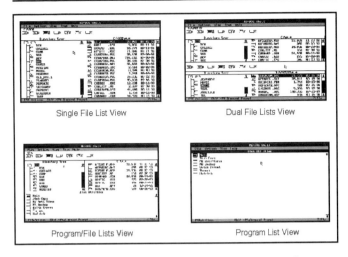

Single File List View

Dual File Lists View

Program/File Lists View

Program List View

Figure 4.2. *DOS Shell can be set to four different views by using the commands on the View menu.*

Using Power Tasks in the Shell

The Shell can be much better than the command prompt interface in daily tasks, such as locating files, selecting files to be processed, and copying and moving files.

Finding a File

Most file-management tasks in the Shell involve selecting files from the file list, and then applying a command to them or dragging them somewhere. The Shell offers several ways to quickly locate the files you want, even if you forget where one or more of them are stored.

Switching Drives Quickly

Opening a drive displays its directory tree and file list on the Shell screen. To open a drive quickly, click the drive icon in the drive list or press Ctrl plus the drive letter; for example, you press Ctrl+D to open drive D.

Refreshing the Drive

The first time you open a drive after starting the Shell, DOS reads the entire directory structure, which it saves in memory. As you add and delete directories and files, the Shell updates the saved directory structure to keep it current. The next time you open the same drive, the Shell saves time by displaying the saved structure, which provides both the tree information and the file list, instead of rereading the drive itself. As long as the Shell can keep accurate track of all the changes you make to the drive, this system works perfectly.

Problems occur when you add and delete directories and files from a temporary command prompt or from an application, where the Shell cannot track the changes. If you see that the directory structure is out of date when you return to the Shell, or if you cannot find a directory or file you just created, you can force the Shell to reread the drive by *refreshing* it. Press F5 to refresh the drive that is open. To refresh a drive as you open it, highlight it and press Enter (instead of the space bar) or double-click it (instead of simply clicking it).

Finding the Right Directory

When you first see the directory tree, it shows only the first level of subdirectories, sorted in alphabetical order. Directories with lower-level subdirectories are identified by a plus sign. When the focus is in the directory tree, typing a character moves the highlight to the next visible directory whose name starts with that character. This is often the fastest way to scroll to the right section of the directory tree.

Clicking the plus sign reveals the next level of subdirectories. The plus sign turns into a minus sign, which you click to hide the subdirectories again. For multiple levels of subdirectories, it is faster to use the keyboard shortcuts on the Tree menu (see fig. 4.3). The fastest way to see an entire branch, no matter how many levels of subdirectories it has, is to move the highlight to it and press *, for example. The fastest way to display the entire directory tree is to press Ctrl+*. You can see more of a long directory tree by choosing View Single File List.

Note: In discussing menu commands, the first word identifies the menu name. The phrase View Single File List means the Single File List command on the View menu.

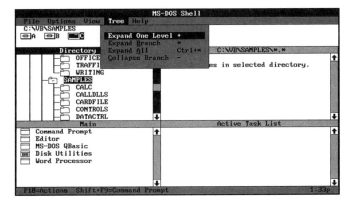

Figure 4.3. *The commands on the Tree menu, which control the appearance of the directory tree, all have keyboard shortcuts.*

Finding a Misplaced File

If you are not sure which directory contains your file, choose View All Files to display all the files on the drive in one list. Figure 4.4 shows what the display looks like. Place the focus in the file list and press the first character of the desired file name to jump to that part of the list. (Duplicate file names occur in the list when the same file name appears in more than one directory.) You usually can see the file you want once you are in the right area. Highlight a file and press F9 to view its contents.

To the left of the file list is an information box. You need it to find out what directory a file is in, especially if multiple files have the same name. The first section of the information box shows the name and attributes of the highlighted file. (This is the last file you selected or, in certain cases, deselected.) The next section (Selected) shows how many files are selected on the current drive and the preceding drive you worked with. The Size field shows the total size of the selected files on both drives. You learn how to use this information later in this chapter.

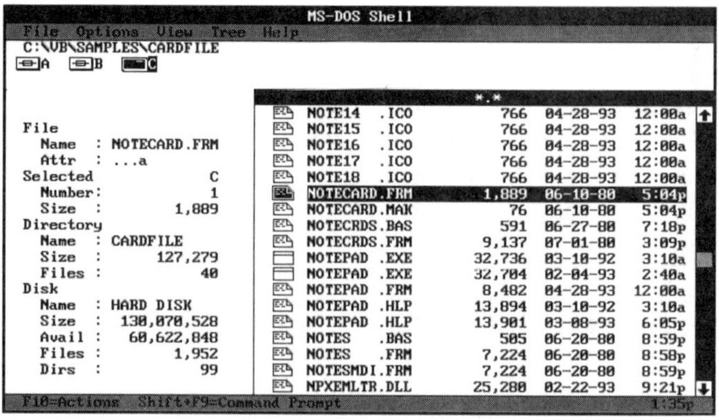

Figure 4.4. *The View All Files command displays all the files on the drive in one list on the right and the information box on the left.*

The third section (Directory) shows the name of the directory containing the highlighted file. It also shows you the total number of files in that directory and how many bytes they add up to. What it does not show you is the full path of the directory, but you can see that at the top of the screen, just above the drive list. The final section (Disk) shows you various statistics for the current drive.

Filtering the File List

If there are too many files for comfort in the file list, choose Options File Display Options to enter a file name filter (see fig. 4.5). You can enter a specific file name such as MYRESUME.PRT or a global name such as MY*.*.

Figure 4.5. *In the File Display Options dialog box, you can enter a file name filter to limit the entries in the file list.*

Displaying Hidden and System Files

Sometimes you cannot find a file because it has a hidden or system attribute. Choose Display Hidden/System Files to add hidden and system files to the current file list. Only those files that match the file name filter will be displayed.

Warning: Most programs assign the hidden and system attributes to protect essential files. Displaying hidden and system files gives you the opportunity to process the files—even to delete them. For the most part, you should not display such files unless you are looking for a missing file. Remove them from the display as soon as possible.

Sorting the File List

Another technique that may help you find a mislaid file is to sort the file list using some other criterion than the file name. Suppose that you created a file this morning and now you cannot remember what you named it or where you stored it. Sorting by date in descending order puts all files created today at the top of the file list. It should be much easier to find the file you want that way.

Using the File Search Command

The File Search command offers another way to find a missing file if you know its name (or at least part of its name). File Search enables you to enter a specific or global file name and choose to search the current directory or the entire drive. Figure 4.6 shows how it displays the search results. This display shows you the full filespec of every found file, a definite advantage, but unfortunately it does not show you the other directory information—size, date/time stamp, and attributes. Highlight a file and choose Options Show Information to see the same information box shown in figure 4.4, and press F9 to see the contents of the highlighted file.

Using Other Search Techniques

If you have no idea what the name of the file is and need to search the contents of your files for a key phrase, such as "Capitol," you will not be able to continue your search in the Shell. Get to the DOS prompt and use the FIND command.

If the file is truly missing, not just mislaid, you may need to undelete it or restore it from a backup copy.

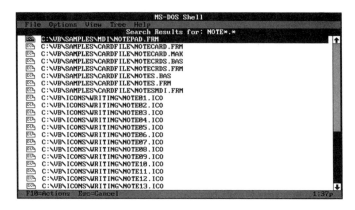

Figure 4.6.   *The Search Results dialog box shows the results of a File Search command.*

Selecting Multiple Files in the Same Directory

Many operations, such as move, copy, and delete, can be done on multiple files. To select several files in one directory using a mouse, click the first file, and then press Ctrl while you click each of the other files. Pressing the Ctrl key while clicking a file selects or deselects it without affecting other selections. (If the desired file names are contiguous, click the first file, and then press Shift and click the last file. All the files between will be selected.)

When you are selecting multiple files, be sure to scroll with the mouse instead of the keyboard. If you press one of the cursor keys, such as PgDn or End, you will clear all the current selections and select the file the highlight lands on.

If you don't have a mouse, you can select adjacent files by holding down Shift while you move the highlight. To select non-adjacent files, you must press Shift+F8 to enter ADD mode, where you can move the cursor without clearing the current selections. Press the space bar to select or deselect the highlighted file in ADD mode. Press Shift+space bar to select all the files between the last file you selected and the highlighted file.

If you are selecting files from a long list, you may want to choose View Single File List so that you can see more of the list at once. You also may want to use Options File Display Options to shorten the file list via a file name filter.

You may be able to use a file name filter to limit the file list to just the files you want. Pressing Ctrl+/ selects all the listed files. Even if it selects a few unwanted files, it may be faster to select them all and use Shift+Click to deselect the ones you don't want.

Note: Ctrl+\ deselects all files except the high-lighted one.

Selecting Files in More than One Directory

The Shell offers two ways to select files in more than one directory. You can view all files and select from the single file list, as shown in figure 4.4, or you can turn on Options Select Across Directories and select from individual directories. The View All Files method is considerably safer for a couple of reasons:

■ When Options Select Across Directories is on, changing directories does not cancel selections in the former directory. If you turn it on in directory A, and then switch to directory B, the highlighted file in directory A remains selected—whether you intentionally selected it or not! You could accidentally delete, move, or copy this file along with the ones you intentionally select.

■ There is no visual clue that alerts you when Options Select Across Directories is turned on; you may forget to turn it off and continue selecting files from multiple directories without realizing it. On the other hand, the View All Files screen looks so different, you will not forget that it is on.

Moving and Copying Files by Dragging

The easiest way to move or copy files is to drag them to the target location. By default, dropping the files on another directory on the same drive moves them, but dropping them on a different drive copies them. You can override the default action by pressing Alt to move the files or pressing Ctrl to copy them.

Make the target location visible before you start so that you have some place to drop the files. You can scroll the directory tree and hide or reveal lower level directories as needed to make a desired target directory visible. If the directory is on another drive but is

not the default directory on that drive, choose View Dual File
Lists and set up the second file list with the desired target
directory.

Deciding whether the Target Disk Has Enough Room

It is unfortunate, but the Shell does not automatically tell
you how many bytes you have selected or how much space is
available on a drive. You have to use the Options Show
Information feature to see these figures.

If you want to know whether a group of selected files will fit on a
target disk, select the files first, switch to the target disk while
being careful not to select any files, and choose Options Show
Information. Figure 4.7 shows an example of this technique. The
Selected section shows that 45,473 bytes are selected on drive C.
The Disk section shows that the current drive, which is drive A,
has 1,212,416 available bytes. The files should fit.

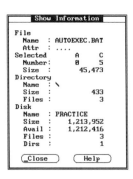

Figure 4.7. *The Selected section of the Show Information dialog
box shows the number of bytes in selected files and the amount of
available space on the currently selected drive.*

Be aware that the files may not fit, even though the target disk
appears to have enough available bytes. Unless you're working
with a DoubleSpace drive, DOS allocates disk space to a file in
blocks called *clusters.* The cluster size is different from disk to
disk, but a typical floppy disk has 512 bytes per cluster, and a
typical hard disk has 2,048 bytes per cluster. If you copy a
10-byte file to a hard disk with 2,048-byte clusters, it takes up
2,048 bytes on the drive. If you copy a 513-byte file to a floppy
with 512-byte clusters, it takes two clusters, or 1,024 bytes. So
whether the files shown in figure 4.7 will actually fit on the

target disk depends on the number of files, their individual sizes, and the cluster size of the target disk.

Options Show Information reports actual file sizes—not the amount of space they take up on the source disk. If the drive is a Double Space volume, the available space is a DoubleSpace estimate based on the current compression ratio.

Note: The CHKDSK program reports the cluster size of a disk. Look for the statistics on *allocation units*, which is another name for *clusters*.

Launching Programs

DOS Shell offers several ways to launch a program. Pressing Shift+F9 gives you a command prompt screen from which you can run programs just as you do outside the Shell. The EXIT command returns you to the Shell; you will have to refresh any drives that you changed from the command prompt.

The File Run command opens a dialog box into which you can enter a single command (see fig. 4.8). You can combine two or more commands by separating them with semicolons surrounded by spaces, as shown in the figure. You cannot run DOSKEY macros from this dialog box.

Figure 4.8. *The Run dialog box enables you to combine two or more commands with semicolons.*

You also can launch a program from the file list by opening its EXE, COM, or BAT file. This method gives you no opportunity to specify parameters or switches. Programs that require parameters, such as FORMAT, will fail when you try to launch them this way. To open a file, double-click it or highlight it and press Enter.

Launching a Data File

There are two ways to launch a program by launching a data file. The first is to drag the file and drop it on the COM, EXE, or BAT file. If you drop AUTOEXEC.BAT on EDIT.COM, for example, the DOS editor starts up with the AUTOEXEC.BAT file open for editing. You cannot change drives or directories while you drag, so both files must be in the same list or you must use the Dual File List view. If both files are in the same list, you can scroll the list in the middle of dragging by positioning the mouse pointer over the up or down arrow at the end of the scroll bar.

If a data file is *associated* with a program, you can launch the program simply by opening the data file. By default, all TXT files are associated with EDIT.COM. If you open README.TXT, the DOS editor starts with the README.TXT file open. All BAS files are associated with QBASIC by default. The Shell has no other default associations.

Tip: Use the File Associate command to set up your own file associations.

Launching from the Program List

Note: See "Defining Your Own Program List," later in this chapter, for instructions on defining your own program list items.

The program list contains items that have been defined, much like batch programs, so that you can launch them simply by opening the items. Depending on how the item is defined, it may use default parameters or it may display dialog boxes to collect parameter information. Figure 4.9 shows what happens when you open the Editor item, which appears on the default program list provided by DOS. After you press the OK button in the dialog box, DOS's full-screen editor (EDIT.COM) starts with the indicated file open.

Figure 4.9. *The File to Edit dialog box appears when you select Editor from the program list.*

Task Swapping

One of DOS's most powerful features enables you to start several tasks at once and switch between them. When you switch from task A to task B, task A remains open. When you return to task A, nothing has changed; the cursor is still in the same location in the same file, waiting for your next action.

If you use Windows, you are familiar with multitasking, which enables you to run several programs simultaneously, perhaps viewing them all at once with several windows open on the desktop and copying data from one to the other via the Clipboard. DOS Shell's task-swapping feature does not have this kind of power. You can see and work with only one program at a time. All other open programs are on hold; they can do no processing until you switch back to them. There is no Clipboard and no way to copy data from one program to another. Still, if you don't have Windows, DOS's task swapping is better than nothing.

Choose Options Enable Task Swapper to start task swapping. When it is on, an active task list appears on your screen (see fig. 4.10). Every program that you launch appears in the list until you specifically terminate it. If you launch more than one copy of the same program, a dot appears next to the name of the second program, two dots appear next to the third, and so on.

To switch to a program, open its item in the active task list or use the keys shown in table 4.1.

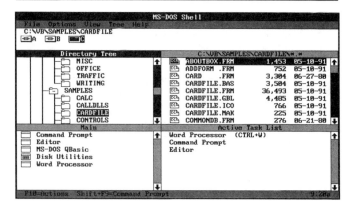

Figure 4.10. *The active task list appears when Options Enable Task Swapper is selected; all currently open programs appear on this list.*

Table 4.1.   Task-Swapping Keys

Key	Function
Ctrl+Esc	Switches to the Shell screen.
Alt+Esc	Switches to the next program in the active task list; does not change the order of the list.
Shift+Alt+Esc	Switches to the preceding program in the active task list; does not change the order of the list.
Alt+Tab	Switches to the next program in the active task list; moves that program to the top of the list.
Shift+Alt+Tab	Switches to the preceding program in the active task list; moves that program to the top of the list.
Alt+Tab+Tab+...	Cycles forward through the task list; when you reach the program you want, release the Alt key; moves that program to the top of the list.
Shift+Alt+Tab+Tab+...	Cycles backward through the task list; when you reach the program you want, release the Alt key; moves that program to the top of the list.

If a program has a task-swapping hot key listed next to it in the active task list (see the Word Processor program in fig. 4.10), you can switch directly to it from any other program by pressing the hot key.

Note: Some programs suppress task swapping; once you start them, you must terminate them before you can access the Shell screen or other programs. Other programs suppress one or more of the task-swapping hot keys because they use those keys for their own purposes.

Defining Your Own Program List

The program list offers the most powerful way to launch programs. You can define separate program groups to delineate major functions or users, and you can define as many program items as desired for the tasks you do on a daily basis. To define a new group or item, place the focus in the program list and choose File New.

Recognizing Password Protection for What it is Worth

The Shell enables you to assign a password to a group or an item. You must provide the same password when you try to open the group or item. The problem is that the passwords are listed in the programstarter section of the DOSSHELL.INI file, which anyone can inspect and change. The Shell disguises the password slightly when it stores it in DOSSHELL.INI, but, to make matters worse instead of better, the disguised form works as well as the original password.

Password protection prevents naive users from accessing program groups and items not meant for them, but it will not block even a mildly experienced person. Anyone who has peeked in DOSSHELL.INI knows how to find out, and potentially change, the passwords.

Using Batch Programs and Combined Commands

You must define a command in the Command box. You can specify only one command for a program item, but you can

combine two or more commands by separating them by
semicolons surrounded by spaces (see fig. 4.11). You can enter
up to 255 characters in the box, although each individual
command should not have more than 127 characters.

Another way to execute multiple commands from a program
item is to create a batch program and execute that from the
program item.

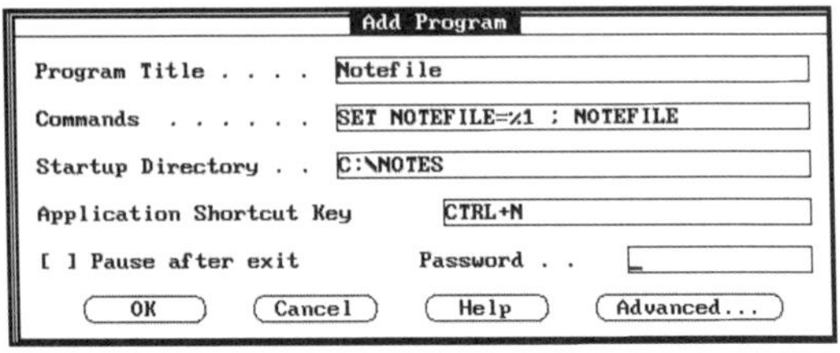

Figure 4.11.   *The Add Program dialog box showing combined*
commands in the Commands field.

Defining an Application Shortcut Key

Some programs start, accomplish a task, and terminate with little
or no interaction from the user. CHKDSK, FORMAT, and
TREE are prime examples. You probably will never find a reason
to switch away from such a program before it terminates, and
there is no reason to set up an application shortcut key for it.

Programs that continue until you specifically terminate them are
another matter. Editors, word processors, database managers,
graphics developers, and similar programs present prime
candidates for task swapping. When setting up a program list
item for such a program, consider assigning it an application
shortcut key. The shortcut key makes it easier to switch to the
program. If you assign Ctrl+Shift+W to Microsoft Word, for
example, you can switch directly to Word (after you have opened
it) from any other open application. If you open more than one
copy of Word, the shortcut key cycles through them.

Place the cursor in the Application Shortcut Key field and press
F1 to see a list of invalid key combinations.

To define a shortcut key, place the cursor in the Application
Shortcut Key field and press a key combination. You must use
the Ctrl, Shift, or Alt key in combination with another key. You
can combine Ctrl, Shift, or Alt plus another key—for example,
Shift+Alt+F5. You cannot use the arrow keys or special keys,

such as Esc and Caps Lock. When you press a valid combination, an expression such as ALT+SHIFT+G appears in the dialog box. DOS Shell does not warn you if another program item uses the same shortcut key combination.

Note: The program starter section of DOSSHELL.INI documents the shortcut key for each program item.

Defining Dialog Boxes for Numeric Variables

When you include a replaceable parameter, such as %1, in a program list command, the Shell enables you to define a dialog box to collect the variable information for that command, such as the one you saw in figure 4.9. You can supply a title for the dialog box, a message for the top, a prompt, and a default value.

The Shell provides some special codes you can use for the default value. The code %F fills in the name of the currently selected file at run-time as the default. The %L code fills in the same value that was used the last time this item was opened.

Defining Memory Requirements

The memory fields in the Advanced dialog box control how much memory the DOS Shell allocates to a program during task swapping (see fig. 4.12). Conventional memory and extended (XMS) memory are handled differently. The regular part of DOS loads programs initially and determines how much conventional and upper memory to give them, but DOS Shell controls all extended memory allocations. When you switch away from a task, the Shell records the program's conventional and upper memory in a disk file so that as much space as possible can be made available to the incoming task. But it simply freezes any extended memory belonging to the task; if the incoming program needs extended memory, the Shell allocates a different chunk to it. When you switch back to a task, the Shell reloads that program's conventional and upper memory from disk and reactivates the extended memory belonging to it.

As you can see, the amount of disk space and extended memory
your saved programs take up determines how many tasks you can
load and swap. In fact, you can run into a situation in which you
cannot switch away from a task until you free some disk space.
Also, the amount of data that must be saved from one program
and reloaded for the next determines how long it takes to swap
tasks.

By default, DOS Shell saves on disk a minimum of 128K of
conventional and upper memory for a program no matter how
much space the program actually needs. You can trim the
amount of disk space used by task swapping and speed up
swapping time if you specify a smaller amount for your program
items in the Conventional Memory KB Required field. This field
does not influence how much space DOS originally allocates to
the program—just how much is saved on disk and reloaded.

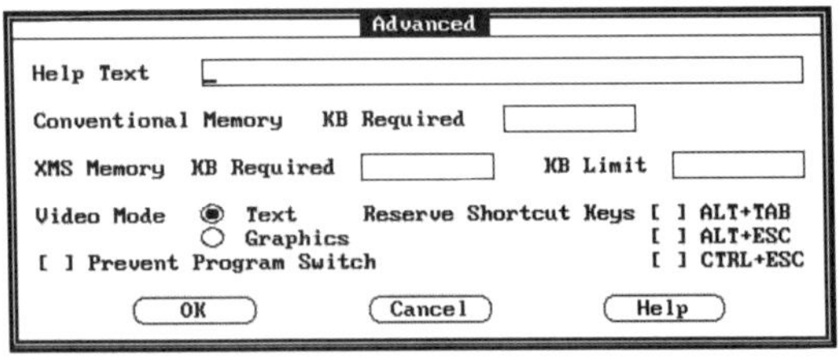

```
┌────────────────────────────────────────────────────────────┐
│                          █ Advanced █                        │
│  Help Text    └                                            ┐ │
│                                                              │
│  Conventional Memory   KB Required    [            ]         │
│                                                              │
│  XMS Memory  KB Required    [          ]    KB Limit         │
│                                                              │
│  Video Mode   ◉  Text      Reserve Shortcut Keys [ ] ALT+TAB │
│               ○  Graphics                        [ ] ALT+ESC │
│  [ ] Prevent Program Switch                      [ ] CTRL+ESC│
│            (     OK     )    ( Cancel )    (  Help  )         │
└────────────────────────────────────────────────────────────┘
```

Figure 4.12.   *The Advanced dialog box defines memory require-
ments (among other things) for DOS Shell's program list.*

You can find out how much conventional and upper memory a
program actually needs by starting it and entering the command
MEM /M *program-name*, as in **MEM /M WORD**. Figure 4.13
shows an example in which the DOSSHELL program requires a
total of 4,640 bytes in conventional memory. For this purpose,
count upper memory along with conventional memory.

The XMS memory fields control how much extended memory
DOS Shell allocates to the program. By default, the Shell
allocates a minimum of 0K and a maximum of 384K (or the
maximum amount of extended memory). The Shell reserves the
full 384K in case the program dynamically requests more
extended memory. If you know that a program requires less than
384K of extended memory, fill in the actual amount needed in
XMS Memory KB Limit to make more extended memory
available to other tasks.

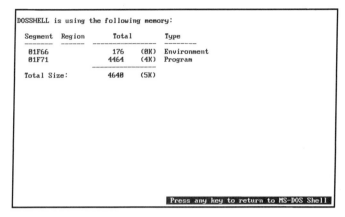

```
DOSSHELL is using the following memory:

Segment  Region      Total        Type
-------  ------    ---------      ------
 01F66                176   (0K)  Environment
 01F71               4464   (4K)  Program
                   ---------
Total Size:          4640   (5K)
```

```
                       Press any key to return to MS-DOS Shell
```

Figure 4.13. *A sample report produced by MEM /M showing the number of bytes that a program takes in memory.*

You also can save memory space by always setting Video Mode to Text. Use Graphics mode (which requires more memory) only if you are using a CGA board and are having trouble swapping tasks. Specifying Text mode here does not prevent you from using graphics mode in the application; it just controls the amount of memory that is set aside.

Controlling Task Switching

If you don't want people switching away from the program you are defining, check Prevent Program Switch. If task switching is OK but the program uses one or more of the task switching hot keys for its own purposes, you can reserve the key for the program's use by checking ALT+TAB, ALT+ESC, or CTRL+ESC. If you don't, the task-switching functions take precedence over the program's own functions.

Tailoring the Shell

There are a few things you can do to personalize the Shell beyond defining your own program items and file associations. You can create your own color scheme or turn off delete confirmation, for example.

Using the DOSSHELL Command Switches

Note: Look up DOSSHELL in DOS's on-screen Help system for a description of its command switches.

If you cannot even get started in DOS Shell because its default display is incompatible with your monitor, you can add switches to the DOSSHELL command to control the initial display mode and color scheme. The following command, for example, starts DOS Shell in low-resolution text mode and a black-and-white color scheme:

```
DOSSHELL /T:L /B
```

After you have started the Shell and can access its menus, use Options Display and Options Color to select the best display mode and color scheme for your monitor. These selections are recorded in DOSSHELL.INI and thus are used for all future sessions. (The command line switches such as /T and /B are not recorded in DOSSHELL.INI.)

Defining Your Own Color Scheme

You can define your own color scheme if the ones provided by DOS don't suit your monitor. Open DOSSHELL.INI with any text editor, such as DOS's EDIT. Find the section named programstarter and look for the color scheme definitions (see fig. 4.14 for an example). Follow the same format to devise your own scheme or edit an existing scheme using the eight basic colors (Black, White, Red, Yellow, Blue, Cyan, Green, and Magenta) and the eight bright colors (Brightblack, Brightwhite, and so on).

Warning: Be sure to read the warning at the beginning of DOSSHELL.INI. It tells you not to let your editor word wrap long lines.

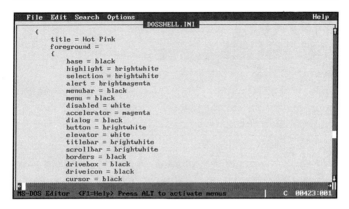

Figure 4.14. *The beginning of the Hot Pink color scheme definition from the programstarter section of DOSSHELL.INI; this foreground section is followed by a background section (not shown).*

Turning Off Confirmation

You can turn off DOS Shell's confirmation features, but they offer good protection even for the experienced user (see fig. 4.15). You may want to turn off Confirm on Delete for a single operation in which you are deleting a large group of files so that you don't have to confirm each one individually. If you do so, be doubly sure that you have selected the correct files and no others, especially if you are using Select Across Directories.

Figure 4.15. *The Confirmation dialog box (Options Confirmation command) is used to control the Shell's three confirmation features.*

Similarly, you may want to turn off Confirm on Replace if you are moving or copying a large group of files and you want them to replace files in the target directory.

Working with
DOSSHELL.INI

As you have seen throughout this chapter, the Shell uses DOSSHELL.INI to store information about the current setup of your Shell screen. You can share your setup—including your program list—with others by copying your DOSSHELL.INI to their computers.

You also can set multiple versions of DOSSHELL for your own computer. You can create DOSSHELL.JNF for one user, DOSSHELL.DNT for another, and so on. They could have different color schemes, different program lists, different file associations, and so on. DOS 6's multiple configuration feature (explained in Chapter 6) helps to determine which DOSSHELL file you want each time you boot. Copy that file as DOSSHELL.INI with a command in AUTOEXEC.BAT before you start the Shell. (Do not just rename it, or the original file will not be available the next time you boot.)

Part II

MAKING DOS WORK SMARTER

5

Conquering Memory

DOS's memory limitations stem from the architecture of the first PCs, which could accommodate only 1M of memory space. An early decision divided that 1M into approximate thirds, giving roughly two thirds (640K) to programs (called *conventional memory*) and reserving about one third (384K) for hardware use (called *upper memory*). This setup is ingrained so deeply into DOS that it is impossible to modify it without changing the very nature of the operating system, making it incompatible with earlier versions and the thousands of applications that have been developed for them.

That 640K memory limit, which seemed so generous at the time, has become DOS's biggest headache. More and more device drivers and terminate-and-stay-resident programs (TSRs) consume permanent space at the same time that applications demand increasing room. Expanded and extended memory provide some relief, but they have their own limitations.

Expanded memory (EMS) is a separate memory device that appears like any other piece of hardware and can be controlled through upper memory; any computer in the PC line can increase its memory space by adding expanded memory. But because DOS cannot address expanded memory directly—it must go through an expanded memory device driver—you cannot load and run programs there, only data files.

Extended memory (XMS) is the memory area above the 1M line in a 286 or higher machine; the machine can address this area directly but DOS cannot. When you are running DOS on a computer with extended memory, you must access the extended area via a device driver, much like expanded memory, and you cannot load or run programs from it. DOS includes its own extended memory device driver, called HIMEM.SYS, that you learn to use in this chapter.

Because of a quirk in the way DOS was designed, it can directly address roughly the first 64K of extended memory. This area is called the *high memory area* (HMA), and HIMEM enables you to load and run one program from it. Most people load DOS there to make sure that a good-sized program gets moved out of conventional memory.

With the advent of DOS 5, the EMM386 driver can load and run programs in unused areas of upper memory, called *upper memory blocks* (UMBs). You may be able to load most of your device drivers and TSRs into upper memory, freeing many kilobytes of conventional memory space. Because the unused UMBs don't have any actual memory chips associated with them, EMM386 remaps portions of extended memory so that DOS can reach it using addresses in the upper memory range. EMM386 runs only on a 386 or higher machine. There are some third-party utilities that accomplish similar functions for a 286. (It cannot be done on an original PC, based on the 8088 chip, because that machine cannot have extended memory.)

Another service provided by EMM386 is to emulate expanded memory. Many programs require expanded memory, but most modern machines have only extended memory. You can ask EMM386 to convert some of your extended memory into expanded memory. You can turn this feature on and off so that you can create some expanded memory just long enough to run one application, and then return it to extended memory again.

Loading HIMEM

The following two commands load the HIMEM.SYS driver and place DOS into the HMA. These commands belong in the CONFIG.SYS file:

```
DEVICE=C:\DOS\HIMEM.SYS
DOS=HIGH
```

Note: Look up HIMEM.SYS in DOS 6's on-screen Help system for the exact format of HIMEM's switches.

HIMEM includes several switches to handle abnormal situations. You probably don't need any of them, but you should be aware that they exist. If, for example, you load HIMEM from the first command in CONFIG.SYS and load DOS into the HMA in the second command, you probably will not need the /A20CONTROL switch, which tells HIMEM to seize control of the HMA if some other program is using it, or the /HMAMIN switch, which establishes a minimum size for a program that can use the HMA.

Depending on your hardware, you may need the following switches:

Switch	Function
/EISA	Machines with EISA architecture and more than 16M of extended memory need this switch.
/CPUCLOCK	HIMEM affects the clock speed of some machines; if your computer malfunctions after loading HIMEM, try including /CPUCLOCK:ON on the command line.
/INT15	If some of your older programs will not work with HIMEM, and especially if you get any messages about INT 15, try including the INT15=nnnn switch on the HIMEM DEVICE command. (You will have to figure out what value to fill in for nnnn; start with 64 and work up in increments of 64.)
/NUMHANDLES	If some of your programs complain about not having enough extended-memory block handles available, use this switch to allocate more handles.
/MACHINE	If DOS cannot access your HMA, HIMEM might be loading the wrong A20 handler software for your hardware. Use the /MACHINE switch to tell HIMEM what computer you have.

You also may want to take a look at the /SHADOWRAM switch. If you are short on RAM and your machine shadows

ROM automatically, HIMEM might try to turn off shadow
RAM, which slows your machine down. If you notice a slow-
down, try including /SHADOWRAM:ON to the command that
loads HIMEM.

Note: EMM386 can also be used to turn shadow
RAM on or off, as you will see later.

Dealing with the Packed File Corrupt Message

When you load DOS into the HMA, you free the first 64K of
conventional memory for other programs. But some programs
don't expect to be loaded that low and issue a `Packed file
corrupt` message. This problem is easily fixed by inserting the
word **LOADFIX** in front of the command to force the program
to be loaded above the 64K line.

Using Upper Memory
Blocks

The following two commands load EMM386 to provide upper
memory blocks. These commands belong in CONFIG.SYS,
right after the commands that load HIMEM.SYS. (EMM386
will not load if HIMEM has not been loaded.)

```
DEVICE=C:\DOS\EMM386.EXE NOEMS
DOS=UMB
```

You can combine the DOS=HIGH and DOS=UMB commands
so that only three commands are needed to load HIMEM, load
EMM386, and move DOS up into the HMA:

```
DEVICE=C:\DOS\HIMEM.SYS
DEVICE\C:\DOS\EMM386.EXE NOEMS
DOS=HIGH,UMB
```

Note: Look up EMM386.EXE in DOS's on-screen Help system to see what parameters are available.

EMM386 has a wealth of parameters, some for its UMB function and some for its expanded memory function. The NOEMS switch, as its name implies, suppresses the expanded memory function so that only the UMB service is provided. You probably will not need any other parameters unless you want to emulate expanded memory.

Loading Programs into Upper Memory Blocks

To load a driver into a UMB, use DEVICEHIGH instead of DEVICE in your CONFIG.SYS file. All DEVICEHIGH commands must come somewhere after the command that loads EMM386. The following command, for example, loads the ANSI.SYS driver into upper memory:

```
DEVICEHIGH=C:\DOS\ANSI.SYS
```

Note: You cannot load HIMEM or EMM386 into upper memory.

To load any other type of program into a UMB, place LOADHIGH or LH in front of the command that you normally use to start the program. Generally, it is better to load TSRs in upper memory along with your drivers. Then you will have the maximum amount of space in conventional memory for transient programs. In AUTOEXEC.BAT, place **LH** in front of every command that starts a TSR. The following commands, for example, load DOSKEY and VSAFE into upper memory, using a few optional parameters for demonstration purposes:

```
LH DOSKEY /BUFSIZE=1024 /INSERT
LH VSAFE /2+ /4- /NX
```

Note: VSAFE normally loads 22K into conventional memory and 22K into extended or expanded memory. The LOADHIGH command affects only the first 22K. Use /NE or /NX to prevent VSAFE from loading into expanded or extended memory, respectively. LH then loads all 44K of VSAFE into upper memory.

Note: SMARTDRV loads itself into upper memory automatically, if it can. You don't need to modify its command(s).

Using MEMMAKER to Squeeze More Programs into Upper Memory

If a program will not fit into upper memory, DOS ignores DEVICEHIGH or LOADHIGH and loads the program into conventional memory. Most computer configurations don't have any trouble fitting everything into upper memory, but if you make heavy use of drivers and TSRs, you may find that they all will not fit.

Note: The MEM command is discussed in detail later in this chapter.

After you modify CONFIG.SYS and AUTOEXEC.BAT and reboot, use MEM /C /P to find out where your programs are. In the example shown in figure 5.1, 15K of DOS, HIMEM, EMM386, COMMAND.COM, and a program called SNAP occupy conventional memory. SETVER, DOSKEY, and SMARTDRV are loaded into upper memory. 514K of conventional memory and 123K of upper memory are available.

```
Modules using memory below 1 MB:

Name          Total      =   Conventional   +   Upper Memory

MSDOS         15437   (15K)       15437   (15K)          0    (0K)
HIMEM          1168    (1K)        1168    (1K)          0    (0K)
EMM386         3120    (3K)        3120    (3K)          0    (0K)
COMMAND        2912    (3K)        2912    (3K)          0    (0K)
SMAP         105920  (103K)      105920  (103K)          0    (0K)
SETVER          640    (1K)           0    (0K)        640    (1K)
DOSKEY         4144    (4K)           0    (0K)       4144    (4K)
SMARTDRV      28320   (28K)           0    (0K)      28320   (28K)
Free         652384  (637K)      526656  (514K)     125728  (123K)

Memory Summary:

Type of Memory       Total      =      Used      +       Free

Conventional        655360   (640K)     128704  (126K)     526656  (514K)
Upper               158832   (155K)      33104   (32K)     125728  (123K)
Adapter RAM/ROM     393216   (384K)     393216  (384K)          0    (0K)
Extended (XMS)     7181200  (7013K)    2323344 (2269K)    4857856 (4744K)

Press any key to continue . . .
```

Figure 5.1. *Sample MEM report showing which programs are loaded into conventional memory and which are loaded into upper memory.*

The MEMMAKER program analyzes your drivers and TSRs and fits them into upper memory as efficiently as possible. It may be able to squeeze more programs into upper memory than you can with standard DEVICEHIGH and LOADHIGH commands. MEMMAKER takes time and can cause problems, so don't use it unless you need to cram your programs into upper memory.

Getting Ready for MEMMAKER

MEMMAKER reads and edits CONFIG.SYS and AUTOEXEC.BAT, and SYSTEM.INI if you use Windows, converting any commands that load drivers or TSRs into DEVICEHIGH and LOADHIGH commands. MEMMAKER adds switches to each command to dictate the exact address where the program should be loaded. Therefore, you need to set up CONFIG.SYS and AUTOEXEC.BAT with all the programs you want to load before running MEMMAKER. If you add a driver or TSR later, you have to run MEMMAKER again to fit the new program in with all the others. (If you will be using Windows, you also need to install it and all its applications first so that SYSTEM.INI is complete.)

Tip: If you have already tried loading programs into upper memory, you don't need to edit the DEVICEHIGH and LOADHIGH commands out of CONFIG.SYS and AUTOEXEC.BAT. MEMMAKER works around them.

Running MEMMAKER

When you are ready, enter the command **MEMMAKER** and follow the directions on-screen. MEMMAKER may need to reboot one or more times as it tries out configurations. It is possible for it to get stuck in the middle of rebooting; you will have to restart the computer to continue (MEMMAKER will still be in control after the cold start). At the end, MEMMAKER displays a report showing how much memory space it has saved, if any. You can choose to keep the new configuration or return to your former one. It reboots one more time and you are up and running with the new (or old) configuration.

Customizing MEMMAKER

At this point, you may discover that the new configuration does not work for you. You may notice problems with your entire system or with certain programs. You may want to try a custom MEMMAKER run, in which you make some of the decisions instead of letting MEMMAKER use its default values. When you choose to customize MEMMAKER, you can make choices such as the following:

- You can exclude individual drivers and TSRs from being loaded into upper memory. This may be necessary if you have a program that does not seem to work well in upper memory.

- You can turn on the Aggressive Scan option so that MEMMAKER tries to load programs into the address range from F000H to F7FFH. This range is normally reserved for ROM BIOS but MEMMAKER will use it if you want. Try turning off the Aggressive Scan option again if your system generally does not seem to work after running MEMMAKER. (If your system locks up during MEMMAKER's reboot, MEMMAKER suggests more conservative settings, including turning this option off—you should agree to do so.)

- You can choose whether to use the region of upper memory reserved for monochrome or Super VGA monitors. If you don't have either type of monitor, you may be able to cram a few more programs into upper memory.

■ If you have already set up EMM386 to include or exclude certain areas of upper memory via switches on the command that loads EMM386, you can ask MEMMAKER to observe the current inclusions and exclusions. By default, MEMMAKER ignores them and the results may not work well on your system.

■ You can try moving the Extended BIOS Data Area (EBDA) to upper memory. This saves some more bytes in conventional memory if it works, but it can cause problems in some systems. If you try this tactic and experience problems with your system, rerun MEMMAKER again and turn this option off.

Note: If you use Microsoft Windows on a 386 with extended memory and a Super VGA display, the MONOUMB.386 file can save you even more space. See README.TXT for details on how to use this file with MEMMAKER.

Undoing MEMMAKER

If you decide to just get rid of all the work MEMMAKER has done, enter the command

MEMMAKER /UNDO

MEMMAKER saves your original AUTOEXEC.BAT, CONFIG.SYS, and SYSTEM.INI. The /UNDO switch restores those original files.

Emulating Expanded Memory

Some programs require expanded memory; others don't require it but will run more efficiently if it is available. If you have such a program but have only extended memory, EMM386 can use some of the extended memory to emulate expanded. If you want to load EMM386 to provide expanded memory services only, not UMBs, omit both the NOEMS and RAM switches from the EMM386 command. If you want both services, use the RAM switch instead of NOEMS.

Note: You don't need to specify an address range with the RAM switch, even though the Help system shows the format as RAM=*mmmm-nnnn*. Just use the word RAM and EMM386 will use all available upper memory space.

Controlling the Memory Size

Note: Look up EMM386.EXE in the DOS on-screen Help system to see the parameters and switches you can use when loading this driver. Not all the switches are discussed in this section.

By default, EMM386 provides a minimum of 256K of expanded memory, which any program can expand up to the complete amount of available space in extended memory or 32M, whichever is smaller. When that program releases the expanded memory, all but the minimum returns to extended memory. You can control the minimum and maximum amounts. The following command loads EMM386 to provide a minimum of 1M of expanded memory and a maximum of 3M:

```
DEVICE=C:\DOS\EMM386.EXE MIN=1024 3072
```

Controlling the Location of the Page Frame

EMM386 establishes a 64K *page frame* in upper memory through which it accesses pages in "expanded" memory just like a real expanded memory driver that adheres to the LIM EMS standard. It may be that EMM386's default location for the page frame is incompatible with your system.

EMM386 gives you several methods of relocating the page frame. The M parameter, the FRAME parameter, and the /P switch all let you identify a specific location in upper memory. The X parameter blocks out a specific area of upper memory for use either as a page frame or as a UMB. The B parameter specifies the lowest address that could be used as a page frame without specifically identifying an address. The method you use depends on your system and what you are trying to accomplish. You might have to do a bit of research on your hardware and BIOS to establish which areas are "safe" and which are to be avoided.

Taking Advantage of Reserved Areas

By default, certain areas of upper memory, such as the range from F000H to F7FFH, are reserved and EMM386 will not try to use them. You may or may not be able to use these areas on your machine for UMBs and page frames. If you have plenty of upper memory space, you might as well leave them alone. If you are running out of space and would like to try some of the reserved areas, run MEMMAKER instead of trying to do it yourself. MEMMAKER tries to do an aggressive setup, which means that it uses some of the reserved areas, and warns you if that does not seem possible. You can access many of these areas yourself by using the B and I parameters, but you will need to know exactly what you are doing.

Note: It is possible to create an EMM386 command that freezes your system during booting. Chapter 6 shows you how to bypass CONFIG.SYS commands during booting so that you can get your system back.

Turning EMM386 On and Off

If you are loading EMM386 just to provide expanded memory for one program, and not to provide UMBs, you don't really need to take up memory room with it until you are ready to run the program. You can use the AUTO switch so that EMM386 is loaded only when a program requests it and is unloaded automatically afterwards.

If you prefer, you can control the loading and unloading of
EMM386.EXE yourself. Use the OFF switch to prevent
EMM386 from being loaded at boot time, then use the com-
mand EMM386 ON when you are ready to load the driver.
When you are done with it, use EMM386 OFF to unload it
again.

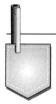

Note: The EMM386 command is different than the
DEVICE command that loads EMM386.EXE. If you
want to look it up in the DOS documentation, look
up EMM386, not EMM386.EXE.

Examining Memory

The MEM command reports on memory usage. In its basic
form, it simply displays a summary of what is currently in
memory, as in the following report:

```
Memory Type       Total =            Used  +       Free
----------------  ------             ------         ------

Conventional      640K               51K            589K

Upper             0K                 0K             0K

Reserved          384K               384K           0K

Extended (XMS)    7168K              2112K          5056K

----------------  ------             ------         ------

Total memory      8192K              2547K          5645K


Total under 1 MB  640K               51K            589K


Largest executable program size   588K (602400 bytes)

Largest free upper memory block    0K      (0 bytes)

MS-DOS is resident in the high memory area.
```

Most of this report is clear, but a couple of lines might be
confusing. The Reserved line shows the total address space
available in upper memory. (In older versions, this line is labeled

`Adapter RAM/ROM`.) The `Upper` line shows how much of it is available for UMBs. In the example, EMM386 has not been loaded so no upper memory is available. This is confirmed near the bottom of the report, where it says that the largest free upper memory block is 0K.

Look how this report changes when EMM386 is loaded to provide UMB support:

Memory Type	Total=	Used +	Free
Conventional	640K	22K	618K
Upper	155K	32K	123K
Reserved	384K	384K	0K
Extended (XMS)	7013K	2269K	4744K
Total memory	8192K	2707K	5485K
Total under 1 MB	795K	55K	741K

```
Largest executable program size   618K (632480 bytes)
Largest free upper memory block    79K  (80512 bytes)
MS-DOS is resident in the high memory area.
```

Now you can see that EMM386 is making 155K of upper memory space available for program use. Of that, 123K is currently available, but the largest block is only 79K. The largest program you can load into upper memory in this configuration is 79K. Notice that EMM386 borrowed 155K from extended memory to fill in the gaps in upper memory; the first report shows 7,168K of extended memory, but the second shows only 7,013K. Notice also the increase in available conventional memory because several drivers and TSRs have been moved to upper memory.

The report changes even more dramatically when you create some expanded memory with EMM386. For the following report, the NOEMS switch was changed to RAM, causing EMM386 to create a minimum of 256K of expanded memory in addition to its UMB functions:

Memory Type	Total =	Used +	Free
Conventional	640K	22K	618K
Upper	91K	32K	59K
Reserved	384K	384K	0K
Extended (XMS)*	7077K	2533K	4544K
Total memory	8192K	2971K	5221K
Total under 1 MB	731K	55K	677K

Total Expanded (EMS)	7488K	(7667712 bytes)
Free Expanded (EMS)*	4784K	(4898816 bytes)

* EMM386 is using XMS memory to simulate EMS memory
  as needed.

  Free EMS memory may change as free XMS memory
  changes.

Largest executable program size	618K	(632480 bytes)
Largest free upper memory block	59K	(60064 bytes)

MS-DOS is resident in the high memory area.

As you can see, upper memory is reduced by 64K, the size of the
page frame, and the largest UMB is now only 59K. That 64K is
added into the size of extended memory, where an attached note
reminds you that EMM386 may be converting extended
memory into expanded. The report also shows sizes for expanded
memory, based not on how much space is currently converted
but on how much could potentially be converted. This depends
on the amount of available extended memory and the maximum
size for the expanded memory conversion.

Getting a Complete Program List

The /C (for Classify) switch causes MEM to report on all the programs currently loaded in memory, except for MEM itself. Refer to figure 5.1 for an example. If the report runs too long to fit on your screen, add /P (for Page) to break it into pages.

Note: In earlier versions of MEM, the /P switch produces a different report and there is no paging function. You can pipe the output to MORE to page it.

The /D (for Debug) switch provides more detail than /C, showing what is in each portion of conventional and upper memory, as shown in the example that follows:

```
Conventional Memory Detail:
```

Segment	Total		Name	Type
00000	1039	(1K)		Interrupt Vector
00040	271	(0K)		ROM Communication Area
00050	527	(1K)		DOS Communication Area
00070	2656	(3K)	IO	System Data
			CON	System Device Driver
			AUX	System Device Driver
			PRN	System Device Driver
			CLOCK$	System Device Driver
			A: - C:	System Device Driver
			COM1	System Device Driver
			LPT1	System Device Driver
			LPT2	System Device Driver
			LPT3	System Device Driver

			COM2	System Device Driver
			COM3	System Device Driver
			COM4	System Device Driver
00116	5072	(5K)	MSDOS	System Data
00253	10096	(10K)	IO	System Data
	1152	(1K)	XMSXXXX0	Installed Device=HIMEM
	3104	(3K)	EMMXXXX0	Installed Device=EMM386
	1488	(1K)	FILES=30	
	256	(0K)	FCBS=4	
	512	(1K)	BUFFERS=15	
	448	(0K)	LASTDRIVE=E	
	3008	(3K)	STACKS=9,256	
004CA	80	(0K)	MSDOS	System Program
004CF	2640	(3K)	COMMAND	Program
00574	80	(0K)	MSDOS	-- Free --
00579	272	(0K)	COMMAND	Environment
0058A	160	(0K)	MEM	Environment
00594	88608	(87K)	MEM	Program
01B36	543888	(531K)	MSDOS	-- Free --

```
Upper Memory Detail:
```

Segment	Region	Total		Name	Type
......	....	.....		....	....
0C93A	1	608	(1K)	IO	System Data
		576	(1K)	SETVERXX	Installed Device=SETVER
0C960	1	48	(0K)	MSDOS	-- Free --
0C963	1	96	(0K)	MSDOS	-- Free --
0C969	1	4144	(4K)	DOSKEY	Program
0CA6C	1	28320	(28K)	SMARTDRV	Program

```
0D156      1  60064(59K)    MSDOS        -- Free --
```

Memory Summary:

Type of Memory	Total =	Used +	Free
Conventional	655360(640K)	22784(22K)	632576 ➡(618K)
Upper	93296(91K)	33088(32K)	60208 ➡(59K)
Reserved	393216(384K)	393216(384K)	0(0K)
Extended (XMS)*	7246736(7077K)	2593680(2533K)	4653056 ➡(4544K)
Total memory	8388608(8192K)	3042768(2971K)	5345840 ➡(5221K)
Total under 1 MB	748656(731K)	55872(55K)	692784 ➡(677K)

Handle	EMS Name	Size
0		060000

```
Total Expanded (EMS)    7667712 (7488K)

Free Expanded (EMS)*    4898816 (4784K)
```

* EMM386 is using XMS memory to simulate EMS memory
➡as needed.
Free EMS memory may change as free XMS memory
➡changes.

```
Memory accessible using Int 15h       0    (0K)
```

```
Largest executable program size   632480  (618K)
Largest free upper memory block    60064   (59K)
MS-DOS is resident in the high memory area.

XMS version           3.00; driver version  3.09
EMS version           4.00
```

With this report, you can see exactly where each portion of each
program is stored and its exact size. Suppose that you want to
find out the effect of adding another 15 buffers; do they go into
conventional memory or into the HMA with the rest of DOS?
Notice that the buffers now take up 512 bytes in conventional
memory. After increasing the BUFFERS command to 30 and
rebooting, you see this line in the MEM /D report:

```
512    (1K)    BUFFERS=30
```

Because they still take up 512 bytes in conventional memory, the
extra buffers must have gone into the HMA. (It is true, they do.
Only if there is not enough room in the HMA are the requested
buffers placed in conventional memory.) You can use similar
techniques to examine the effects of various configurations on
your system's memory usage.

Taking Another Look at Memory Use (and More) with MSD

The MSD (Microsoft Diagnostics) program provides another
interesting look at memory use, and other diagnostic information as well. Figure 5.2 shows the main menu that appears when
you start MSD. As you can see, MSD provides reports on your
computer itself, memory, various pieces of hardware, TSRs, and
so on. These reports provide more detail than you need for
everyday tasks, but if something is wrong in your system, a
Microsoft engineer may request information from one or more
MSD reports.

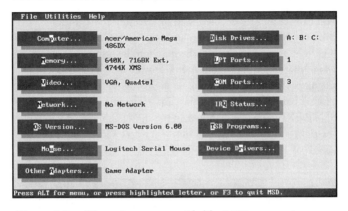

Figure 5.2. *The main menu provided by MSD summarizes your current memory usage, among other things.*

Memory usage is summarized next to the Memory button. You can select the Memory button to see more details on each of these memory areas, including a somewhat primitive map of upper memory (see fig. 5.3). In the figure, you can see the upper portion of the map, from address C000H to address FFFFH. You can see that ROM is at C000H to C7FFH and at F000H to FFFFH, and so on. (The report displayed by the Utilities Memory Browser command shows that the ROM at C000H is the Video ROM BIOS and the ROM at F000H is ROM BIOS.)

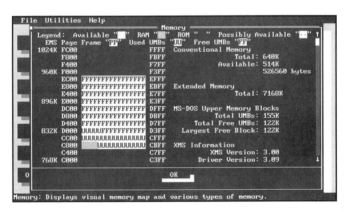

Figure 5.3. *MSD's memory report showing details about various sections of memory and a map of upper memory.*

You can see a more detailed map by selecting the Utilities
Memory Block Display command (see fig. 5.4). As you move the
highlight around in the list, the map scrolls to show you exactly
where that block is located. A **⊢** symbol marks the block on
the map. (If the block is small enough, you will see only the two
vertical bars, not the connecting line.) The location of the
SNAP.EXE program is shown in the figure. The two columns to
the right of its name tell you that it starts at address 0595H for a
length of 105,728 bytes.

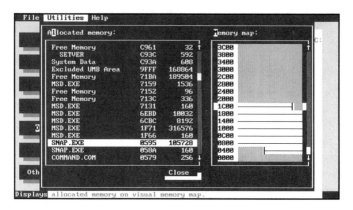

Figure 5.4. *The Utilities Memory Block Display map gives more
details about the location of specific programs in memory.*

Most of the time, you will not need the detailed level of information provided by MSD; MEM is sufficient to tell you what's
loaded where and how much space you have left. But if you ever
do need the extra details, you know where to find them.

6

Adding Power to Your Boots

DOS 6 has added several powerful new features to give you more control over the boot process. You can now display a menu during the processing and choose from a variety of setups. And you can bypass all or part of CONFIG.SYS and AUTOEXEC.BAT during booting.

Setting Up Multiple Configurations

DOS 6 enables you to set up multiple configurations in CONFIG.SYS so that you could, for instance, create a different configuration for each person who uses your computer or for your major applications. Figure 6.1 shows an example of a boot menu as displayed by CONFIG.SYS. The user's choice on this menu determines which block of CONFIG.SYS commands is executed.

Creating the Menu

The following commands create the menu shown in figure 6.1. No matter where you place these commands in CONFIG.SYS, they are executed first.

```
[MENU]
SUBMENU=Judi
MENUITEM=Greg
MENUITEM=Davida
MENUITEM=OTHER, None of the above
MENUCOLOR=3
MENUDEFAULT=Judi,5
```

When you use multiple configurations, all commands are placed in *blocks* headed by [*name*]. The [MENU] header identifies the block of code that defines the menu. The SUBMENU and MENUITEM commands define the menu options. In the case of Judi, Greg, and Davida, the name of the item is also the text that appears on the menu, because no other text is defined. The fourth item is named OTHER, but the displayed message is `None of the above.`

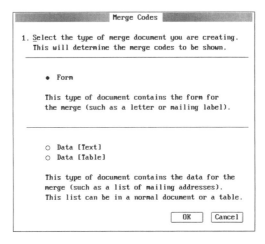

Figure 6.1. *A menu displayed during execution of CONFIG.SYS.*

Note: On the menu, DOS displays whatever case you specify in the SUBMENU and MENUITEM commands but otherwise ignores case when processing the commands.

The MENUCOLOR command establishes the screen colors for the menu display, in this case cyan text on the default background color. The MENUDEFAULT command sets up Judi as the default menu choice and five seconds as the time-out time; if the user does not respond to the menu within five seconds, the default choice is assumed.

Creating a Submenu

The SUBMENU command defines an item that, if chosen, leads to another menu. In this case, the second menu is named JUDI, and DOS looks for a block headed by [JUDI] for the definition of the submenu. The submenu block also would contain MENUITEM commands as needed to establish the submenu, perhaps defining MENUCOLOR and MENUDEFAULT as well.

Defining Command Blocks

In the example, the rest of CONFIG.SYS would be composed of blocks headed by [GREG], [DAVIDA], [OTHER], and whatever other names are established by the [JUDI] submenu. Each of these blocks would contain whatever CONFIG.SYS commands are necessary to set up the desired configuration for the selected option.

Establishing a [COMMON] Block

If any commands are shared by all options, such as DEVICE=C:\DOS\HIMEM.SYS, you can create a [COMMON] block for them. Common blocks are executed before the selected option block.

Warning: Once you have set up CONFIG.SYS in blocks, you will have to edit it each time you install a new program that might add to it, to make sure that the commands go into the correct block.

Including Other Blocks in a Block

If some commands are common to some blocks but not all blocks, you still don't have to type them more than once. Place them in a separate block and use the INCLUDE command to include them in another block. Suppose that three out of four of your options set up EMM386 for UMBs only. You might create a block like this:

```
[UMBBLOCK]
DEVICE=C:\DOS\EMM386.EXE NOEMS
DOS=UMB
```

In each option block that needs these two commands, you insert the following command:

```
INCLUDE=UMBBLOCK
```

The commands in UMBBLOCK are executed at the point that DOS encounters the INCLUDE command.

Using the CONFIG Environment Variable

Note: Chapter 11 explains environment variables and Chapter 3 explains how to use them in batch files.

DOS automatically sets the CONFIG environment variable to the name of the option chosen during booting. If, for example, you choose Greg during booting, you will find the following variable in the DOS environment:

```
CONFIG=Greg
```

You can use this variable in AUTOEXEC.BAT and other batch programs to process commands appropriate to the selected configuration. The easiest way is to set up a structure like this:

```
REM Start with commands common to all
➥configurations
@ECHO OFF
...
...
REM Branch to the selected configuration
GOTO %CONFIG%

:GREG
REM This section sets up the configuration for Greg
...
...
GOTO ENDING

:DAVIDA
REM This section sets up the configuration for
➥Davida
...
```

```
...
GOTO ENDING

:OTHER
REM This sets up the configuration if the user chose
"None of the above"
...
...
GOTO ENDING
```

In the command GOTO %CONFIG%, DOS substitutes the value of the CONFIG variable for %CONFIG%, so the command that is executed becomes GOTO Greg, GOTO Davida, GOTO OTHER, or whatever. Set up each option to be processed by a block of commands headed by :*label* and terminated by GOTO ENDING to jump past the other blocks. There may be more commands after ENDING that are common to all the configurations.

Bypassing the Configuration Commands

Whenever you make changes to CONFIG.SYS, and to a lesser extent AUTOEXEC.BAT, you take the chance of making a mistake that will freeze the system during booting. Choosing the wrong parameters for EMM386, for example, could lock up your system.

In the old days, once the system was frozen, you could not boot from the hard drive to fix it, and you had to fall back on a bootable disk to get started again. But with DOS 6, you can bypass all or part of CONFIG.SYS and AUTOEXEC.BAT and complete your boot from the hard disk.

Note: If you want to inhibit other people's ability to bypass CONFIG.SYS and AUTOEXEC.BAT, insert the command SWITCHES /N somewhere in CONFIG.SYS. When you do this, no one can bypass the startup files, not even you, and you will have to boot from a floppy if something goes wrong.

Bypassing All Startup Files

To bypass all of CONFIG.SYS and AUTOEXEC.BAT, press
Shift or F5 when you see the message `Starting MS-DOS....`
You will see the message `MS-DOS is bypassing your`
`CONFIG.SYS and AUTOEXEC.BAT files.` If
COMMAND.COM is not in the C:\ or C:\DOS directory,
DOS asks you where to find that file.

Note: DOS pauses two seconds after displaying
the Starting `MS-DOS...` message to give you a
chance to press one of the bypass keys. You can
suppress this pause by inserting SWITCHES /F
anywhere in CONFIG.SYS.

When you bypass the startup files, you bypass commands that
install installable device drivers, your extended or expanded
memory driver, and so on. You probably will want to limp
around in this configuration only long enough to fix the
startup files and reboot.

Bypassing Individual Commands

To bypass individual commands in CONFIG.SYS and
AUTOEXEC.BAT, press F8 during the `Starting MS-DOS`
message. DOS displays each line from each startup file and asks
whether you want to execute it. Suppose that you have just
changed your EMM386.EXE command in CONFIG.SYS and
now your system will not boot. Use F8 to bypass individual
commands and answer Y (for Yes) to every command except
EMM386.EXE. Now most of your configuration is in place, and
it's fairly easy to edit CONFIG.SYS to fix the EMM386.EXE
command.

7

DoubleSpace

The most popular feature of DOS 6.0 is DoubleSpace, the data compression program, but it has resulted in data loss in a few cases. The major purpose of the DOS 6.2 step release is to correct the problem situations with two important new DoubleSpace features:

- SCANDISK identifies and circumvents physical flaws on a drive.

- DoubleGuard prevents corruption of DoubleSpace's memory buffers.

These new features are vital to accurate DoubleSpace performance. If you installed DoubleSpace under DOS 6.0 and haven't stepped up to 6.2, you should do so immediately. If you haven't installed DoubleSpace, be sure to step up to DOS 6.2 before doing so.

Is DoubleSpace now safe? Probably. But any data-compression program can encounter trouble given a specific combination of hardware, drivers, TSRs, and applications. So if you're using another data-compression program, it's problem free, and you're happy with its performance, there's little sense in switching to DoubleSpace. If you haven't yet installed data compression and want to try DoubleSpace, be sure to back up all your data first. And back up often after installing DoubleSpace.

Understanding Data Compression

Data compression works by removing repeated data strings from a file and replacing them with markers that indicate which characters to repeat. As a simple example, suppose that a file contains only the sentence "No news is good news." A data-compression program would replace the second "news" with a marker pointing back to the first "news," saving several bytes of storage space.

The amount of space saved by compression depends on how much repetition a file contains. In a typical system, the overall compression ratio is 2 to 1. That is, for every two characters in the uncompressed file, only one character is stored in the compressed version (hence the name DoubleSpace). But compression ratios can range from around 1.2 to 1 for font files to around 16 to 1 for bit-mapped graphics. So depending on what kind of data you store in your system, you could realize more or less space savings than the typical 2 to 1.

Some compression systems work on a file-by-file basis. If you want to compress a file, you enter a command to do so. When you want to uncompress it, you have to enter a command for that function. PKZIP, from PKWARE, Inc., is the best-known example of this type of program. Its main advantage is its simplicity.

Compression systems such as DoubleSpace work by creating a compressed drive in your system. Any data stored on that drive is compressed automatically. Any data read from the drive is uncompressed automatically. You don't have to enter specific commands to compress or uncompress data. These types of compression systems are much more complex, but once installed and functioning properly, you're less aware of the compression and decompression process.

DoubleSpace Features

DoubleSpace is part of the core of the DOS operating system and is loaded at the same time as the other core programs—IO.SYS and MDDOS.SYS—before CONFIG.SYS. This offers a tremendous advantage over older compression programs, which don't load until CONFIG.SYS is processed. With those programs, some CONFIG.SYS commands must refer to the drives by their unmounted names while others must use the mounted names—all very confusing. With DoubleSpace, the drives are mounted before CONFIG.SYS is processed, and CONFIG.SYS uses only the mounted names.

DoubleSpace can turn an existing drive into a compressed one or create a new drive out of the empty space on a drive. It can also create a compressed drive on a floppy disk. Certain files will not work if they're compressed (such as the Windows permanent swap file). When you compress an existing drive, DoubleSpace automatically bypasses those files and keeps them in the uncompressed host drive.

Mounting and unmounting of hard drives are automatic during booting. With DOS 6.0, you have to mount compressed floppies with a specific command, but with DOS 6.2, floppies also are mounted automatically. Compression and decompression are automatic as you store data in and read it from a compressed drive; in that sense, at least, you will not even be aware of the compression system.

Once you have created a compressed drive, you can maintain it through a graphics interface or at the command prompt. You can expand or shrink the compressed drive as needed, obtain status reports, run SCANDISK on it, and so on.

DoubleSpace interacts with programs that report the amount of available space on a drive, such as DIR and CHKDSK, to estimate the number of uncompressed bytes you can move to the drive instead of the actual number of bytes available. In other words, when DIR reports that there are 20M bytes available on the drive, there are probably more like 10M actually available, but at a 2:1 compression ratio, you will be able to store 20M worth of data there. You see a little later in this chapter how to determine the real amount of space on the drive and how to control the compression ratio that DoubleSpace uses for the estimate.

Updating from Version 6.0

If you installed DoubleSpace under DOS 6.0 and have stepped up to DOS 6.2, you may need some extra steps to continue using DoubleSpace. The step-up program replaced the copy of DBLSPACE.BIN that is in your DOS directory with the newest version, but it may not replace the copy that was stored in your boot directory. If you try to boot with the old version, you may see the message Your computer is running with an incompatible version of DBLSPACE.BIN. To solve the problem, copy DBLSPACE.BIN from the DOS directory to the boot directory, overwriting the version of DBLSPACE.BIN in the boot directory.

Getting Ready to Compress

Your first step in preparing for DoubleSpace, of course, is to decide what you're going to compress. Do you have only one hard drive, or do you have several? Do you want to compress them all or just one? Or do you just want to compress some empty space to create a new drive where you will store compressed data?

If you'd like to try DoubleSpace but you're leery of compressing drive C, you're not alone. Even though DOS 6.2 has made DoubleSpace much safer, there's still a slight chance of something going wrong. As an alternative, you might try compressing another hard drive. If you don't have another drive, try compressing the empty space on drive C. By the way, you cannot just try it out on a floppy. When you install DoubleSpace for the first time, you must compress a hard drive. You can compress floppies only after DoubleSpace has been installed.

Warning: With DOS 6.0, you cannot easily remove DoubleSpace once you have installed it. Don't compress a drive just to find out what happens unless you have DOS 6.2.

You should observe a few precautions before installing DoubleSpace for the first time. If you're going to compress an existing drive, back up all the data. Even with the DOS 6.2 safeguards, DoubleSpace can fail. If you're going to create a compressed drive out of empty space, run DEFRAG to bring all the empty space together. You also may want to delete unwanted files and purge Delete Sentry. You must disable Delete Sentry or any other deletion-protection program while installing DoubleSpace.

Warning: When you install DoubleSpace, you make permanent changes to your system. You can no longer uninstall DOS, unformat the drive, or undo SCANFIX corrections to the drive.

If you're running any disk-caching program other than SMARTDrive, disable it before trying to install DoubleSpace. Microsoft recommends that you delete the command that loads the third-party disk caching program and install SMARTDrive instead.

Finally, read the DoubleSpace section of the README.TXT file before starting compression. It contains any last-minute tips on DoubleSpace. It also tells you how to convert your drives from other compression software, such as Stacker, to DoubleSpace.

Installing DoubleSpace

The first time you use DoubleSpace, you must install it by entering just the word **DBLSPACE** at the command prompt. The first DoubleSpace window appears to guide you through the process.

Express versus Custom Installation

You must choose between express or custom installation. An express installation compresses the existing data on drive C. If you don't want to do that, choose the custom installation option.

Installation Time

Be prepared for a long installation process. It can take quite a while to scan the host drive. If you choose to compress existing data, installation will take even longer as DoubleSpace compresses the data. The DoubleSpace windows keep you informed as the process continues.

Understanding Your New Drive

Figure 7.1 shows how DoubleSpace manages hard drive names, according to whether you compressed existing data or created a new drive out of empty space. When you create a new compressed drive out of the empty space on a host drive, DoubleSpace assigns a new name (not necessarily K) to the new drive. When you compress the existing data on a drive, DblSpace assigns the original drive name to the compressed drive and a new name to the host drive; this way, you don't have to change any programs or batch programs that refer to the files that were compressed. (In most cases, only DOS refers to the files on the host drive, and DOS knows what drive name to use.)

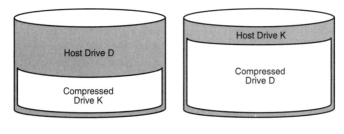

Compressing Empty Space   Compressing Existing Data

Figure 7.1. *The names that DoubleSpace assigns to drives depends on how you create them.*

The new drive is not really a drive at all. It's actually a file called a Compressed Volume File (CVF). DoubleSpace makes this file behave like a drive. If you examine the root directory of the host drive, including hidden and system files, you would see a file named DBLSPACE.*nnn*, as in DBLSPACE.000 or DBLSPACE.001. This is the CVF.

Warning: Don't move, rename, delete, or otherwise touch any file named DBLSPACE.*ext*, or you will lose the ability to access the data on your compressed drive(s).

Mounting and Unmounting

When DOS begins to boot, before DoubleSpace loads, the host drives have their original names and the compressed volumes are just files. When DoubleSpace loads, it *mounts* the compressed drives; that is, it assigns drive names to them, swapping names with the host drives, if necessary. A compressed drive must be mounted before it can be used.

A floppy compressed drive must also be mounted before it can be used. With DOS 6.0, you must enter a command to mount a floppy compressed drive. With DOS 6.2, compressed drives on floppies are mounted automatically when you insert the disk into the drive unit. With both versions, floppy drives are unmounted automatically when you remove the disk.

DoubleSpace includes commands to mount and unmount drives, but you will probably never need to use them.

DBLSPACE.BIN and DBLSPACE.SYS

After installing DoubleSpace, you will notice a new driver added
to your CONFIG.SYS file, called DBLSPACE.SYS. This is not
the DoubleSpace program, which is called DBLSPACE.BIN and
is loaded before CONFIG.SYS is processed. DBLSPACE.BIN
initially loads into the highest part of conventional memory,
leaving room for other programs to load lower down. (Upper
memory blocks are not available until CONFIG.SYS has been
processed.) The sole purpose of DBLSPACE.SYS is to move
DBLSPACE.BIN after the rest of CONFIG.SYS has been
processed, all other drivers are loaded, and upper memory blocks
are available. DBLSPACE.SYS moves the DoubleSpace program
into upper memory, if possible; otherwise, it moves it down as
far as possible in conventional memory.

Note: If you use EMM386.EXE to make upper
memory blocks available, change the DEVICE
command for DBLSPACE.SYS into a
DEVICEHIGH command or run MEMMAKER
after installing DoubleSpace.

Coordinating with the Deletion Protection Files

When you create a new compressed drive on a host drive that is
protected by Delete Tracker, the PCTRACKR.DEL file for the
drive is invalidated and DOS will ignore it. After the compressed
drive is created, Delete Tracker correctly tracks its files as well as
the host drive's files.

If the host drive was protected by Delete Sentry, you will find
SENTRY directories for both the host and the compressed drive.
You probably will not be able to recover any files that were
deleted before the compressed drive was created, but from now
on, Delete Sentry works for both drives.

Coordinating with SMARTDrive

You don't need to change your SMARTDrive setup after
creating a new compressed drive. SMARTDrive caches the host
drive as always; in the process, it caches the compressed drive,
too. Write caching could cause problems on a compressed drive,
so you are better off using read caching on such drives.

Managing Compressed Drives

After the first compressed drive has been installed, DoubleSpace
offers both a graphic interface and a set of commands to create
more drives and to manage your compressed drives. This chapter
shows you how to use the graphic interface. DOS 6's Help
system documents the equivalent commands.

When you enter the command **DBLSPACE** without any
switches, a dialog box similar to the one in figure 7.2 opens. It
lists all your compressed drives.

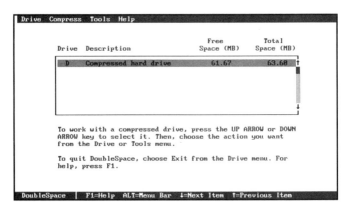

Figure 7.2.   *After DblSpace is installed, the DBLSPACE command opens a dialog box where you can select and manage your
compressed drives.*

Compressing Additional Drives

Pull down the Compress menu to create another compressed
drive. The menu contains two commands, Existing Drive and

Create New Drive. To compress the existing data on a drive, choose Existing Drive. To create a new drive out of empty space, choose Create New Drive. After you have made your choice and identified the host drive, the compression process is just like before.

Tip: If you don't plan to compress any floppy disks, turn off the AUTOMOUNT feature to save about 4K in memory. You can turn it off by choosing the Tools Options command in the DblSpace window (explained shortly) and deselecting the Enable automounting option.

Using DIR with Compressed Drives

You can see your file-by-file compression ratios by adding the /CH switch to the DIR command, as shown in the following example:

```
DIR /CH

 Volume in drive D is HDRIVE D
 Volume Serial Number is 10D9-1A7A
 Directory of D:\TRUST


.          <DIR>              09-03-93   8:40a
..         <DIR>              09-03-93   8:40a
BUDNEWA   BAK    124,788      04-29-93  12:23a   1.5 to 1.0
SCRIPT    STY    512          07-24-90   9:23p   4.0 to 1.0
BUDNEWA   DOC    120,653      08-23-93  10:42a   1.5 to 1.0
FLOOD1    BAK    41,210       08-23-93  10:10a   1.4 to 1.0
FLOOD1    DOC    42,008       08-23-93  10:29a   1.4 to 1.0
          1.5 to 1.0 average compression ratio
          7 file(s)  329,171 bytes
                    64,667,648 bytes free
```

You can see the compression ratio added to each line. The overall compression ratio at the end averages only the files listed, not the entire drive.

Note: If you use /C instead of /CH, DoubleSpace uses a different process to compute the compression ratios, which is not as accurate.

Expanding a Compressed Drive

What happens if you run out of space on a compressed drive? You might be able to expand it if you can find or make room on the host drive. By default, DoubleSpace leaves 2M of space on the host drive when it compresses existing data. It stores any files that should not be compressed in this free space. If you do a custom setup, you can change that when the drive is created. If you created the compressed drive out of empty space, the uncompressed space on the host drive could be any size.

If there is free space on the host drive, you can expand the compressed drive to fill all or part of it. If there is no free space, you might be able to free some by deleting unnecessary uncompressed files from the host drive and moving others to another drive. Don't, however, tamper with DBLSPACE.*ext* or the DOS core program files. In fact, you should probably leave all hidden and system files alone on the assumption that someone gave them the hidden or system attribute for a reason. If you want to move the Windows swap file, use the Windows Control Panel to relocate it; don't just move the file yourself. (And don't place it on the compressed drive.)

Choose the Drive Change Size command to open a dialog box in which you can see information about the host drive and the compressed drive (see fig. 7.3). In the example, the host drive currently has 2M of free space. You make the compressed drive larger by reducing the amount of free space on the host drive. The Minimum Free Space figure in the Uncompressed Drive column shows the smallest amount of free space you can assign to the host drive. In the example, if you want to make the compressed drive as large as possible, you would set the free space on the host drive to 0.13M.

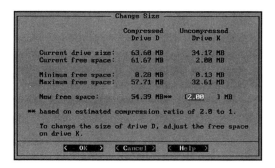

```
                     ┌──────────── Change Size ────────────┐
                     │              Compressed   Uncompressed│
                     │              Drive D        Drive K   │
                     │  Current drive size:  63.60 MB   34.17 MB │
                     │  Current free space:  61.67 MB    2.00 MB │
                     │                                       │
                     │  Minimum free space:   0.28 MB    0.13 MB │
                     │  Maximum free space:  57.71 MB   32.61 MB │
                     │                                       │
                     │  New free space:      54.39 MB** [2.00 ] MB │
                     │ ** based on estimated compression ratio of 2.0 to 1. │
                     │                                       │
                     │  To change the size of drive D, adjust the free space │
                     │  on drive K.                          │
                     │     < OK >    < Cancel >    < Help >  │
                     └───────────────────────────────────────┘
```

Figure 7.3. *The Change Size dialog box displays current size information for the selected compressed drive and its host drive and lets you change the sizes.*

Contracting a Compressed Drive

You may find it necessary to make a compressed drive smaller so that you can store more uncompressed data on the host drive. Before trying to contract the compressed drive, defragment it so that all of its free space is in one chunk. This affects how much space can be removed from the drive. Choose Tools Defragment to defrag the drive.

Note: The only time you need to defragment a compressed drive is when you want to reduce its size.

Then choose Drive Change Size to open the same dialog box shown in figure 7.3. The Maximum Free Space figure in the Uncompressed Drive column shows you how much you can increase the host drive space. Increase the free space value up to this maximum to reduce the amount of space given to the compressed drive.

Scanning a Compressed Drive

You should scan your compressed drive often for errors in the FAT structure and physical flaws. Run SCANDISK on the compressed drive just as you run it on any other drive.

Note: If you started using DoubleSpace with DOS 6.0, you may have used the CHKDSK function on the Tools menu to check your compressed drive. That function has been disabled in DOS 6.2.

Updating the Compression Ratio

DoubleSpace uses an estimated compression ratio to compute its space estimates for commands such as DIR and CHKDSK. It updates the estimated compression ratio every time it mounts the drive by computing the actual overall compression ratio for the drive. You can force it to update the compression ratio right now by choosing the Drive Change Ratio command (see fig. 7.4).

Figure 7.4.   *The Change Compression Ratio dialog box enables you to update the compression ratio to the actual average or to enter your own estimated ratio.*

The first line of the dialog box shows the current estimate and the second line shows the actual compression ratio. You can enter a new estimated compression ratio to match the actual one.

You may want to enter a different estimate altogether. Some programs depend on DOS's space report to determine whether or not they can store their files on the drive. If they don't see enough space, they issue an error message and quit. If this happens to you and you suspect that there really is enough space on the drive (for example, if the files in question typically compress at a much higher ratio than the current average), you can set a higher ratio and try again.

As an example, many word processors that run under Windows now include extensive clip art libraries. Depending on the graphics format involved, clip art could compress at a ratio anywhere from 4 to 1 to 16 to 1. If you're trying to install such a program and the installation program says there's not enough room for the clip art on the drive, try setting the estimated compression ratio at 5 to 1 (or higher) temporarily.

Note: If your actual ratio is running high because you have stored many graphic files on a drive, it will cause your estimated ratio to be too high and your space available estimates could fool you into thinking you can store more data on the drive than you can. You can counteract this by resetting the ratio every time you boot with a DBLSPACE / RATIO=*n.n* command in AUTOEXEC.BAT.

Viewing Drive Information

The Drive Info command opens a dialog box in which you can examine statistics for the selected drive (see fig. 7.5). You can link from there to the Change Size and Change Ratio dialog boxes by choosing the Size and Ratio buttons.

Figure 7.5. *The Drive Info command displays usage information about the selected compressed drive.*

Removing Compression

You can remove all the data from a compressed drive without removing the drive by deleting all the files or reformatting the drive. Choose the Drive Format command to reformat it. (DOS's FORMAT command will not do it.)

You can delete all a compressed drive's data and eliminate the
drive itself by choosing the Drive Delete command. This also
unmounts the drive so that the host drive resumes its original
name. Deleting all your compressed drives doesn't uninstall
DoubleSpace. It is still loaded every time you boot and takes up
room in memory.

Tip: UNDELETE can recover a deleted CVF.

To uncompress the data on a drive, choose the tools Uncompress
command. There must be enough space on the host drive to
hold all the uncompressed files. You might have to delete files
or move them to other drives to create enough room for the
uncompression process. Depending on the amount of data to be
uncompressed and the speed of your computer, it could take a
long time to uncompress an entire drive.

Tip: Uncompression can encounter problems.
Back up all your compressed files before
uncompressing a drive.

When you uncompress the last mounted drive in your system,
the DoubleSpace program is automatically removed from
memory. If you want to completely uninstall DoubleSpace,
however, you must delete DBLSPACE.BIN and
DBLSPACE.INI from your boot directory. They have hidden
system and read-only, so you will have to remove their attributes
before deleting them. (Don't delete them from the DOS
directory; you may want to reinstall DoubleSpace someday.)
You should also edit CONFIG.SYS to remove the command
that loads DBLSPACE.SYS.

Bypassing DblSpace

If you're having some problems with your system after installing
DoubleSpace and you want to try booting without DoubleSpace,
you can press Ctrl+F5 when you see the `Starting MS-DOS...`
message during booting.

Working with DBLSPACE.INI

The DBLSPACE.INI file contains several parameters that control DoubleSpace options. You can control the maximum number of fragments a CVF can be broken into , for example, as well as the number of floppy drives that DoubleSpace can handle. All these parameters can be controlled by various DoubleSpace commands. (A few can be set by choosing the Tools Options command.) For specific information on the parameters in the DBLSPACE.INI file and how to set them, enter the command **HELP DBLSPACE.INI** at the DOS command prompt.

Part III

POWER TASKS

Managing Files

DOS gives you a number of ways to manage files, but which are the most efficient and which are the safest? This chapter shows you the best and quickest methods available at the command prompt.

Finding a Misplaced File at the Command Prompt

Chapter 4 showed you several ways to locate a misplaced file from DOS Shell. But you don't need the Shell just for that. If you know the file name, or at least the first part of it, you can use the DIR command with the /S and /B switches to locate the file.

Using DIR to Find Files

/S searches all subdirectories of the specified directory, and /B suppresses most of the normal directory information, simply listing filespecs. When /B and /S are used together, DIR adds the complete path to each filespec. Suppose that you cannot find a file but you think its name starts with COMM. The following command lists all files on drive C that match the global file name COMM*.*, as shown in the following sample listing. You can usually identify the desired file from such a listing.

```
C:\>DIR C:\COMM*.* /S /B

C:\COMMAND.COM
C:\DOS\COMMAND.COM
C:\NDW\COMMEXT.DLL
C:\POWERDOS\COMMTEXT.DOC
C:\WINDOWS\FONTBANK\COMMO___.TTF
C:\WINDOWS\SYSTEM\COMM.DRV
C:\WINDOWS\SYSTEM\COMMDLG.DLL
C:\WINDOWS\SYSTEM\COMMO___.FOT
```

This particular search function is so handy that it makes a good
DOSKEY macro. In the following command, the macro receives
the name FF for "find file." The $* parameter includes all
parameters from the invoking command in the macro.

```
DOSKEY FF=DIR /B /S $*
```

Searching for Characters Anywhere in a File Name

Sometimes you know that the misplaced file contains a certain
string of characters in its name, but not necessarily at the
beginning of the name. Suppose that you think the file you
want contains *URB* somewhere in its name. You can search
for all filespecs that contain *URB* by piping the output of the
DIR /S /B command to FIND. In the DIR command, use
. as the filespec so that a complete directory is passed to
FIND.

Be sure to match the cases of the DIR and FIND commands.
DIR produces uppercase by default and FIND is case sensitive
by default. In the URB example, either search for *URB*, use
DIR's /L switch to generate lowercase letters and search for *urb*,
or use FIND's /I switch to ignore case.

The following command finds all files on drive C containing
URB in their filespecs. Notice that the CURB directory is listed,
along with every file in that directory. This happens because
FIND searches for *URB* anywhere in the line. Nonetheless, it is
usually pretty easy to find the file you are looking for.

```
C:\>DIR \*.* /S /B ¦ FIND "URB"

C:\CURB
C:\CURB\REFIG.CB
C:\CURB\CCCMAG.CBS
C:\CURB\CCCLLL.CB
C:\VB\SAMPLES\CARDFILE\SUBURBS.CRD
C:\VB\SAMPLES\CARDFILE\URBANA.$CC
C:\WINDOWS\SYSTEM\COURBD.FOT
C:\WINDOWS\SYSTEM\COURBD.TTF
C:\WINDOWS\SYSTEM\COURBI.FOT
C:\WINDOWS\SYSTEM\COURBI.TTF
```

Again, this makes a pretty handy DOSKEY macro. Add FIND's
/I switch so that you don't have to bother entering uppercase
letters for the $1 parameter, as follows:

```
DOSKEY FX=DIR \*.* /S /B ¦ FIND "$1" /I
```

Copying Files: The Best Way

The best way to move and copy files uses DOS Shell or Windows, because they don't terminate the process when the target disk is full; you get the chance to change floppies and continue. But if you need to move or copy files at the command prompt or in a batch program, use XCOPY instead of COPY.

Choosing XCOPY over COPY

When copying multiple files, XCOPY reads as much as possible into memory, and then writes it to the target directory, whereas COPY reads and writes only one file at a time. XCOPY's technique can be much faster, depending on the number and size of the files you're copying.

XCOPY sets an exit code that you can follow up in a batch program; COPY does not. Also, XCOPY copies from whole branches if requested, creating directories as needed on the target disk; COPY copies from one directory at a time and fails if it cannot find the specified target directory.

Note: When XCOPY cannot figure out whether you want it to create a new file or a new directory, it asks `Does name specify a file name or directory name on the target (F = file, D = directory)?` You must respond with F if you want to create a new file or D if you want to create a new directory.

Moving a Branch

XCOPY combined with DELTREE provides DOS's best method of moving a whole branch. First, use ATTRIB to see whether there are any hidden or system files in the branch. If so, they will not be copied by XCOPY, so you probably want to remove their attributes. Next, copy the entire branch to its new location. Use XCOPY's /S switch to copy all subdirectories of the specified directory; use /E if you want to copy empty directories as well. Finally, delete the branch from its original location.

Suppose that you want to move the WP branch from drive C to drive D. The following three commands accomplish the task as long as there is plenty of room on drive D to hold the branch:

```
ATTRIB C:\WP\*.* -S -H /S
XCOPY C:\WP\*.* D:\WP\ /E
DELTREE C:\WP /Y
```

In the XCOPY command, it is important to specify the target as D:\WP\ so that XCOPY knows to create a new directory named WP as the top of the branch. If you specify the target as simply D:\, XCOPY copies the files from C:\WP into the root directory of D, and then creates the subdirectories of C:\WP under the root directory of D. The D:\WP directory never gets created.

Note: In versions of DOS before 6.2, you must include the /S switch with the /E switch on the XCOPY command.

Tip: When you put a backslash at the end of the target path name, XCOPY knows that it's a directory name and does not have to ask.

Using COPY for Its Other Functions

The COPY command can do a couple of things that XCOPY cannot: it can copy to or from a device, and it can concatenate (combine) files. Both of these functions, however, are better accomplished using other utilities and applications. If, for example, you want to create a short text file by copying from keyboard to disk, use EDIT. Also use EDIT to combine two or more text files. To concatenate word processing documents, use the word processor that created them. The same is true for any data files created by applications, whether they are graphics, spreadsheets, databases, or whatever. To concatenate program files—if you are sure you want to do that—use the linkage editor that came with the program development software.

Moving Files

As mentioned earlier, the best way to move files is through the Shell or Windows. But if you want to move files from the command prompt or a batch file, the MOVE command provides the best way. When you are moving files from one directory to another on the same drive, MOVE merely moves each file's directory entry, not its data. This saves a great deal of time and prevents the possibility of errors creeping in during reading and writing. Also, it means that there is no possibility of a disk-full error.

Renaming Files and Directories with MOVE

The MOVE command also enables you to rename a file or directory. The following command changes the name of C:\THISYEAR to C:\LASTYEAR:

```
MOVE C:\THISYEAR C:\LASTYEAR
```

You also can change a file name using MOVE. If the target directory is the same as the source directory, the file is renamed rather than moved. The following command changes the name of C:\DRIVERS\SHADOW.OLD to C:\DRIVERS\SHADOW.SYS:

```
MOVE C:\DRIVERS\SHADOW.OLD C:\DRIVERS\SHADOW.SYS
```

In both cases, it's important to specify the path for the target name. If you don't and the source is a file, you will end up moving the file to the current directory in addition to renaming it. If the source is a directory, you will get an error message because MOVE cannot move a directory.

Protecting Target Files

With DOS 6.2, COPY, MOVE, and XCOPY are finally able to protect files in the target directory from being overwritten by the new files. If a target file is about to be overwritten, a message similar to the following appears:

```
Overwrite C:\DRIVERS\SHADOW.SYS (Y/N/A)?
```

If you answer **Y**, the existing file is overwritten with the new file. If you answer **N**, the new file is not placed in the directory. In both cases, DOS goes on to the next file to be copied or moved,

which may or may not generate a similar prompt. If you answer
A (for "all"), the existing file is overwritten and the protection
feature is disabled for the remainder of the job. That is, all
remaining files referenced by this command are copied or
moved without checking for existing files.

By default, if you enter the COPY, XCOPY, or MOVE command at the command prompt, target files are protected
automatically. But if a batch file issues a COPY, XCOPY, or
MOVE command, they are not. You can override the default
protection with the /Y switch. /-Y protects files, whereas /Y
doesn't. Suppose that you want to copy all the files from drive B
to C:\CAPCOM, automatically replacing any matching files.
The following command accomplishes this task:

```
XCOPY B:*.* C:\CAPCOM /Y
```

Suppose that, in a batch program, you want to copy
C:\AUTOEXEC.BAT to A:\, but only if there is no
A:\AUTOEXEC.BAT. The following command gives
the user the option of replacing A:\AUTOEXEC.BAT:

```
XCOPY C:\AUTOEXEC.BAT A:\ /-Y
```

If, however, you want to protect A:\AUTOEXEC.BAT without
confusing an inexperienced user with unexpected prompts and
messages, the following command does a better job:

```
IF NOT EXIST A:\AUTOEXEC.BAT XCOPY C:\AUTOEXEC.BAT A:\
```

If you prefer to always have protection on or off, you can set the
COPYCMD variable in the environment. Set it to /Y to disable
protection both at the command prompt and in batch files. Set it
to /-Y to enable protection in both situations. For example, the
following command turns on file protection for all COPY,
MOVE, and XCOPY commands:

```
SET COPYCMD=/-Y
```

When you set up a default with the COPYCMD variable, you
can still override the default on individual commands with the
/Y OR /-Y switch.

Copying Files with REPLACE

> **Note:** Look up REPLACE in DOS's on-screen Help system to see its syntax, notes, and examples.

The REPLACE command offers two special functions that you cannot find elsewhere in DOS. Both functions stem from its capability to select files to be copied by comparing the source directory with the target directory:

■ REPLACE can copy missing files to the target directory; that is, it copies any files that appear in the source directory but not the target.

■ REPLACE can overwrite files in the target directory with files from the source directory; that is, it copies only those files from the source directory that match existing file names in the target directory.

Replacing Missing Files

When you use the /A switch, REPLACE copies missing files to the target. This feature provides an interesting way to copy files without the danger of overlaying identically named files in the target directory. The following command copies from A:\ to C:\WP only those DOC files that don't exist in the target directory:

```
REPLACE /A A:\*.DOC C:\WP
```

Updating Files

Suppose that you update one or more files and want to replace all other copies of those files with the updated versions. REPLACE without /A seeks out and replaces files that have the same name as the files in the source directory. In the following command, the upgraded files are located in A:\, and they are being used to upgrade all other copies of the same files (as indicated by identical file names) throughout drive C:

```
REPLACE A:\ C:\*.* /S
```

If there is a possibility that some of the files to be replaced are read-only, and you want to replace them too, be sure to use the /R switch. REPLACE terminates itself immediately if it tries to replace a read-only file without the /R switch.

Note: REPLACE will not find or replace hidden or system files.

Deciding on UNDELETE

The safest and best way to protect your files is to make frequent backups, store your backups in a safe place, and save them long enough so that you can fall back to files you deleted quite some time ago. Some people keep their backup disks for years; they can restore a file they deleted several years ago, if need be! A good backup system protects your files not only from deletions but also from viruses, hard disk failure, theft, sabotage, and all the other ills that can befall your computer. Chapter 9 discusses DOS's BACKUP and RESTORE programs.

Use UNDELETE only to recover files that have not yet been backed up. If you create a new file today, delete it before backing it up, and then decide that you want it back, UNDELETE may be able to recover it for you. But without Delete Sentry, UNDELETE is basically unreliable; even if it tells you that it can recover a file, it might recover the wrong data into the file. If you plan to use UNDELETE at all, you should install Delete Sentry and set it up to preserve only files that haven't been backed up (that is, files with the Archive attribute). The following procedures show you how to configure Delete Sentry to preserve unarchived files only.

To configure Delete Sentry using the Windows version of Undelete, follow these steps:

1. Open the Microsoft Tools group.

2. Open the Undelete program. (The Microsoft Undelete window appears.)

3. Choose Options Configure Delete Protection. (The Configure Delete Protection dialog box opens.)

4. Select Delete Sentry and press the OK button. (The Configure Delete Sentry dialog box opens.)

5. Select Do not save archived files. (Make sure that the check box contains an X.)

6. Choose OK to close the dialog box. (A message box tells you to reboot.)

7. Choose OK to close the message box.

8. Close the Microsoft Undelete window.

9. Exit Windows.

10. Reboot.

To configure Delete Sentry using the DOS version of Undelete, follow these steps:

1. If you have never installed Delete Sentry protection, install it now by entering the command UNDELETE /S.

2. Edit the file named C:\DOS\UNDELETE.INI.

3. Find the line that starts with ARCHIVE=.

4. Make sure that this line says ARCHIVE=FALSE. If it says TRUE, change it to FALSE.

5. Save the file.

6. If you haven't already done so, edit AUTOEXEC.BAT to start Delete Sentry.

7. Exit the editor.

8. Reboot.

Even Delete Sentry cannot guarantee a file's recovery. Delete Sentry preserves deleted files for a while so that you can recover them with 100 percent reliability. But it purges files after a specific number of days, if its directory gets too full, or if DOS needs disk space to store new data. So you may find that the file you want has been purged from Delete Sentry and cannot be recovered. (You can manually purge files from Delete Sentry, but in the DOS version of UNDELETE, you cannot select files to be purged; it's all or nothing.)

Another problem with the UNDELETE system is that it does not see actions such as replacements made by move and copy as deletions; even when Delete Sentry is in effect, replaced files are not preserved.

Tip: If you are desperate to undelete a file and
UNDELETE cannot do it, try an undeletion
program provided by a third-party utility package,
such as PC Tools or The Norton Utilities. They
enable you to explore the free space on your drive
and recover any data you find there. (If you need
to do this, don't do anything else on your computer until you can run the undeletion utility. Any
other action may overlay the data you need to
recover.)

Warning: Do not try to recover a program file
using UNDELETE without Delete Sentry. An
improperly recovered program could damage
data in your system.

Other Uses for DELTREE

At last, you can delete an entire branch without deleting each
directory individually. Of course, caution is necessary. With
DELTREE, you can end up deleting many files you did not
intend to. But a power user is always a careful user.

The beauty of DELTREE is not just that it deletes whole
branches in one command. There are many more deletion
tasks you can handle better with DELTREE than with DEL.

Deleting a Single Directory

Note: Look up DELTREE in DOS's on-screen
Help System to see its syntax, notes, and examples.

You don't have to apply DELTREE to an entire branch. It can just as easily delete a single directory without making you delete all the files first. The following command deletes the A:\OLDVAULT directory, whether or not it has subdirectories. The /Y switch prevents DELTREE from displaying a confirmation prompt before deleting the directory.

```
DELTREE /Y A:\OLDVAULT
```

Note: DELTREE is fussy. You have to put the /Y switch before the path name or file name.

Deleting Files Regardless of Attributes

When you want to delete a branch, you specify the path name of the branch in the DELTREE command. But suppose that you include a filespec instead of or in addition to the path name? In the directory that heads the branch, DELTREE deletes only those filespecs that match the filespec. For lower level directories, it deletes those directories that match the filespec; it does not delete individual files from the lower levels.

DELTREE's advantage over DEL for deleting individual files is that it ignores attributes. DELTREE deletes hidden, system, and read-only files as well as normal ones—obviously a feature that you should use with a great deal of caution. The following command deletes all the BAK files in the current directory, regardless of attributes. In this case, the /Y switch prevents DELTREE from listing each file for confirmation. (It also deletes any subdirectories of the current directory that match the *.BAK filespec, which is not likely to happen.)

```
DELTREE /Y *.BAK
```

Deleting with Multiple Filespecs

Another advantage of DELTREE over DEL is that it permits multiple filespecs. The following command deletes all the BAK and SAV files in C:\WP, regardless of attributes. (It also deletes all subdirectories of C:\WP that match the *.BAK and *.SAV filespec.)

```
DELTREE /Y C:\WP\*.BAK C:\WP\*.SAV
```

You can include as many filespecs as needed, up to DOS's 127-character limit for commands.

Clearing a Directory

DELTREE cannot delete the current directory, although it can delete all its files and subdirectories. When you apply DELTREE to the current directory using the *.* file name, it deletes all the files from the current directory, and it deletes all its subdirectories and their files, thus clearing the current directory. The following command clears the current directory without prompting for confirmation:

```
DELTREE /Y *.*
```

You can clear an entire disk by applying this command to the root directory.

Deleting Specified Subdirectories

Suppose that your WP branch looks like this:

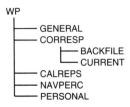

Suppose that you want to delete all subdirectories except GENERAL and PERSONAL. You can specify the exact subdirectories that you want to delete. If WP is the current directory, the command looks like this:

```
DELTREE CORRESP CALREPS NAVPERC
```

As with all branches, deleting CORRESP automatically deletes its two subdirectories.

Group Renames

Sometimes it is handy to be able to rename a whole group of files with one command. If you are careful, you can rename an entire set of files with one command at the command prompt using the REN command. (MOVE cannot accomplish this task.)

The group rename feature works well when you just want to change file extensions. The following command renames all NOW files in the current directory as OLD files:

```
REN *.NOW *.OLD
```

The following command assigns the name OLD to all the files in the current directory, no matter what extension they had before:

```
REN *.* *.OLD
```

Note: This command will fail if any file in the directory already has the OLD extension. Any file names that follow the one with the OLD extension are not renamed. It also will fail if two or more files have the same name but different extensions; the first one will be renamed to *filename*.OLD, but the second one will cause the command to fail.

It is almost as simple to replace the beginnings of a set of file names. The following command renames all files that start with NOW in the current directory so that they start with OLD instead:

```
REN NOW*.* OLD*.*
```

The following command replaces the initial character of each file name in the current directory with X, no matter what the initial character was before:

```
REN *.* X*.*
```

Note: This command will fail because of a duplicate file name if any file name in the current directory already starts with X. Any files following the one that starts with X are not renamed. It will also fail if two files have the same name except for the first character, as in FREE.TXT and TREE.TXT.

The following command selects all files starting with CD and replaces the first four characters of the file name with DISC. That is, CDROM changes to DISCM, CDREADER changes to DISCADER, and so on:

```
REN CD*.* DISC*.*
```

If you try to get any more complex than the preceding command, you might end up with file names you did not want. DOS will process a command such as REN ?BAT*.?X? XXX*.293, but you may not like the results.

Getting More out of FC

Note: Look up FC in DOS's on-screen Help system to see its syntax, notes, and examples.

When you need to compare two files, FC does a much better job than the old COMP, especially if you want to know not just if they are different, but how. For ASCII comparisons, FC displays the lines that don't match and tries to resynchronize the files again after the mismatch so that the comparison can continue.

Note: COMP was dropped with DOS 6, but you still may have a copy in your DOS directory if you upgraded from an earlier version of DOS. You can safely delete it; FC is a much better program.

Comparing Two Source Code Files

Suppose that you have two versions of AUTOEXEC.BAT on your hard drive and you want to see how they are different. In this case, you want to identify the differences in effect, not just do a character-by-character analysis. The commands PROMPT PG and prompt pg are logically identical, even though one is uppercase and the other lowercase. In this case, you probably want to use the /C switch to ignore case. If you are comparing program source code files, such as two BAS files, where indentation is often used to show structure, you also may want to use the /W switch to ignore white space (spaces and tabs).

Comparing CONFIG Files

Comparing CONFIG.SYS files can be slightly tricky because FC automatically uses binary mode on SYS files, which are usually program files. But CONFIG.SYS is a text file. If you want to see a line-by-line display of how two CONFIG.SYS files differ, use the /L switch to force FC to use ASCII mode. You will probably also want to use /C to ignore case.

If you are comparing CONFIG.SYS to a file named something like CONFIG.OLD or CONFIG.SAV, you don't need the /L switch if you put the other file first in the command. When two files have different extensions, FC uses the first extension to determine the default mode of the comparison. The following command results in a binary comparison:

```
FC CONFIG.SYS CONFIG.OLD
```

But the following command results in an ASCII comparison:

```
FC CONFIG.OLD CONFIG.SYS
```

Tip: If mismatches are found, FC probably generates more lines of information than will fit on your screen. Pipe the output to MORE or redirect it to PRN so that you have the chance to read it.

Trying to Find a Rematch

When FC encounters a mismatch in the two files, it searches ahead in both files trying to find a place where they match up again. It continues the comparison from that point on. This way, you can find out all the differences in the two files, not just the first one. If FC fails to resynchronize the two files after a mismatch, you will see the message `Resynch failed.`
`Files are too different.`

When FC is trying to locate a rematch, it fills its resynch buffer with lines from both files. Then it searches the buffer for matching lines. If it cannot find matching lines in the buffer, it gives up. It does not refill the buffer with more lines from the files and continue trying. So it might not compare all of the files.

By default, the resynch buffer can hold 100 lines from each file. You can increase that amount with the /LB*nnn* parameter. If two files fail to resynchronize within the default 100 lines, try adding /LB200 to the command line and rerunning the comparison. You will see the message FC: Out of memory if you request a larger buffer than FC can fit into memory.

9

The New MSBACKUP

Your backup program is one of the most important programs in your system because it serves to protect your files from any kind of damage. DOS 6's MSBACKUP (and its Windows equivalent MWBACKUP) is a vast improvement over the old BACKUP and RESTORE commands. The new backup program provides a graphical interface and enables you to easily set up a regular backup cycle.

You should back up your files on a regular basis. Most power users back up at the end of each work day; some do it more often than that. Back up often so that you can count on your backups to restore the most current versions of your files no matter what crisis befalls your computer.

You do not need to back up all your files. You already have backups of any applications that you still have the original disks for. And you certainly do not need to back up temporary files, BAK files, and the like. Any files that you can eliminate from the backup save you time and disk or tape space. MSBACKUP enables you to identify a set of files to be backed up. You save your selections in a *backup setup* so that you only have to select them once. (Your entire backup configuration is saved in the setup.)

MSBACKUP automatically creates and maintains a catalog for each backup you make. The catalog identifies every file in the backup. When you want to restore some files, you examine the catalog and select the files to be restored. For convenience, MSBACKUP stores the current backup catalogs on your hard drive as well as the backup disks or tape. It automatically deletes old backup catalogs on the hard drive when you run a new backup, so only the most recent catalogs appear on the hard drive.

This chapter assumes that you have run MSBACKUP or MWBACKUP at least once, so you have completed the required configuration tests and you have used a backup setup. It concentrates on creating the best backup setup for your system and on restoring files.

Selecting the Best Backup Type

BACKUP offers three backup types: full, differential, and incremental. The full type backs up all selected files, whether or not their archive attributes are on. It turns off the archive attributes of all files that it backs up. This is a good way to start off a new backup cycle, say once a week or once a month, depending on how you design your system. It gives you a clean start; you have a good, up-to-date copy of all the selected files, and their archive attributes are all off. As you start modifying and creating files, DOS turns on their archive attributes to indicate that they need to be backed up.

After the full backup, you really do not need to do another one for a while. You save time and disks by doing differential or incremental backups in between full backups. Both differential and incremental backups record only those selected files whose archive attributes are on. The difference between the two types is whether they turn off the archive attributes after backing up the files.

The differential method leaves the attributes on so that the same files (along with any files created or modified in the meantime) will be backed up again the next time you run a backup. When you use a differential system, each backup records all the files that have been created or modified since the last full backup. Each differential backup completely replaces the preceding backup; theoretically, you need to save only the most recent backup disks plus your last full backup to have a complete set of the selected files with which to restore the hard disk. Some people who use differential backups use the same disks every day, overwriting yesterday's backup with today's. The differential backup is the best type to use if you modify the same files every day. If your work consists mainly of constantly updating a database, appointment schedule, or spreadsheet, then the differential method works fine.

But two potential problems arise when you overwrite each day's differential backup with the next day's. First, you cannot fall back to an earlier version of the same file without going all the way back to the last full backup. This may not be a problem in your work. After you update your database, for example, you may not want to fall back to an earlier version. But if you introduce some errors into the database and do not notice it for a few days, sometimes going back to an earlier version is the best solution to fixing the problem. (You still need to remake the good entries to bring your database up to date, however.) Second, if you create or update a file after the last full backup and then delete it, it is no longer saved in the differential backups. If you have not saved your earlier differential backups, you will no longer have a record of the most recent version of the file.

For these reasons, it is not a good idea to eliminate your differential backups too soon. Many cautious users save all differential backups at least until the next full backup; others save them for much longer because they want to be able to go back to earlier versions and to recover deleted files. If you're going to do this, consider using the incremental backup type instead.

The incremental backup turns off archive attributes after recording the selected files. Each backup records only the files you worked on since the last backup. You save all the incremental backup disks at least until you do the next full backup.

The incremental backup is the best method to use if you create and modify many different files on a daily basis. If word processing is your main task, for example, then the incremental backup is the best type for you.

Whichever method you decide to use, select it in the Backup Type box in the main Backup window. When you're ready to do a full backup, simply switch the Backup Type to Full long enough to make the backup, and then switch it back to Incremental or Differential again.

Choosing the Best Options

Each backup setup includes a set of options that determine how the backup is performed. Figure 9.1 shows the dialog box that opens when you select the Options button in the Backup window. The default options are checked in the figure, but that may not be the best set of options for your setup. You can choose options to give you maximum speed, maximum compression, or maximum protection.

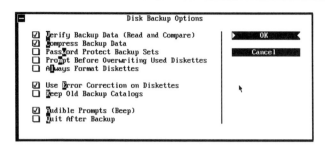

Figure 9.1.   *The Disk Backup Options dialog box opens after you select the Options button in the Backup window.*

The Best Options for Maximum Speed

If you want to keep your backup time as short as possible, choose the Compress Backup Data option. When the data is compressed, it takes about half as many disks, which saves a considerable amount of time both in writing and in waiting for you to change disks. Also turn on Quit After Backup so that MSBACKUP terminates without waiting for you to choose the exit command.

MSBACKUP displays a time estimate in the Backup window based on the amount of data selected, the number of disks that it will take (if disks are involved), and some of the selected options. The Compress Backup Data option does not affect the time estimate (or the space estimate), so if you select this option, mentally lower the time estimate accordingly.

Note: To evaluate the effect of each option, a little more than 1M of data (1,165,061 bytes) was selected, and backups first were run with no options, and then with each option in turn. With no options, the backup took 51 seconds. With data compression, the same backup took only 40 seconds.

All the following options add to the backup time:

- Verify Backup Data. The time it takes to reread, perhaps decompress, and compare the data after it is written adds significantly to the length of the backup. The test backup using this option took 1 minute 15 seconds. This option is counted in MSBACKUP's time estimate.

- Password Protect Backup Sets. MSBACKUP must stop and ask you for a password if you turn on this option. (The time test is invalid here because the time it takes to collect the password is not counted in the backup time.)

- Prompt Before Overwriting Used Disks. When this option is selected, MSBACKUP must check each disk to see whether it contains data; if so, it must display a message and wait for you to respond before it can continue. In the time test, this option increased backup time to 56 seconds (including the time it took to respond to the warning message). It is not counted in the estimated backup time.

- Always Format Disks. This option adds more time to your backups than any other option, because formatting each disk takes considerable time. (MSBACKUP automatically formats unformatted disks anyway. This option causes it to format all disks.) This option increased backup time to 1 minute 32 seconds. It is not counted in the backup time estimate.

- Use Error Correction on Disks. It takes time to create and write the error-correction data. The time test took 56 seconds with this option. It is counted in the backup time estimate, although not accurately.

There are also some hardware decisions you can make to minimize backup time. The fastest backup is to another hard drive, of course, if you have that option available to you. Backing up to another hard drive or to tape means that you do not have to change disks. If you must use floppies, use the drive with the highest capacity to minimize the number of disks required. If you have two identical drives, select the two-drive option so that you can insert the next disk into the other drive while the current drive is being written.

The Best Options for Maximum Compression

If you are more concerned with saving floppy disk space than with maximizing protection, choose Compress Backup Data. Also turn off Use Error Correction on Disks, because the error-correction code takes up about 10 percent of the disk space.

The Best Options for Maximum Protection

Because you back up your files to protect your data, it makes sense to set up your backup options for maximum protection, even if that takes more time and disks. Choose the following options for maximum protection:

- Verify Backup Data. When this option is selected, MSBACKUP rereads all the data it writes, comparing it to the source on hard disk. If MSBACKUP finds errors, it corrects them if possible. Otherwise, it notifies you that the disk is unreliable and asks for another. This option is preferable to running a comparison after the backup is completed because it identifies and corrects for errors as you go. If you do not find out until later that the backup disks are imperfect, you have to rerun the entire backup to correct the disks.

- Prompt Before Overwriting Used Disks. This option warns you if a disk contains any kind of data. If the disk contains an earlier backup, it tells you the date and catalog name of the backup. Using this option can help to prevent accidentally overwriting an earlier backup too soon.

Warning: MSBACKUP overwrites all existing data on the target disk; this data cannot be recovered.

- Always Format Disks. A used disk may have deteriorating sector information; a freshly formatted disk is much more reliable.

- Use Error Correction on Disks. This option causes MSBACKUP to create and store on each disk special error-correction codes that can help it recover data from the disk even if it is physically damaged.

The two most important protection options are Verify Backup Data and User Error Correction on Disks. The former guarantees that the backup is accurate, and the latter helps to recover data even after a disk has been sitting in storage for a year or longer. (All disk data deteriorates eventually.) If you want to run a compromise between minimum time and maximum protection, turn on these two options and turn off all other options.

If you are backing up sensitive data, such as personnel records, and do not want others to be able to access it from your backup disks, you also may want to use Password Protect Backup Sets. This option does not make your backup data any more reliable, but it does prevent access by anyone who does not know the password. (Don't forget your passwords or you will not be able to restore your own files.)

Choosing the Best Way to Select Files

MSBACKUP gives you several ways to select and exclude files, each with its own special effect. You can create include and exclude statements, manually select or deselect individual files and directories, specify special exclusion parameters, and select or deselect entire drives. Include and exclude statements enable you to select files by global filespecs, and, thus, they affect files that you add to your drive in the future as well as the ones that are there now. For the most part, try to do most of your file selection via include and exclude statements. To create an include or exclude statement, choose the Select Files button to open the Select Backup Files dialog box, and then choose the Include or Exclude button (see fig. 9.2).

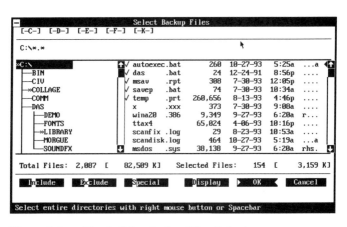

Figure 9.2. *Use the Select Backup Files dialog box to create include and exclude statements, to manually select files and directories, and to specify special exclusions.*

Avoid manual selection or deselection unless you are positive about a particular file or directory. Manual selection, in which you double-click or press Enter for a file or directory in the Select Backup Files dialog box, overrides the include and exclude

statements forever for that file or directory. Even if you deselect
the file or directory again, it becomes manually deselected and is
still not affected by the include and exclude list. You can
eliminate all manual selections by deleting the file named
setup.SLT.

Tip: You don't have to scroll through the entire
file list to see which files are selected if you choose
the Display button and choose Group Selected
Files. This option places all selected files at the
beginning of the file list.

Don't be fooled by the name of the Special Selections dialog box
(see fig. 9.3). It does not select files—it merely excludes them. If
you apply a date range from 8-1-92 to 8-1-94, for example, you
exclude any files from outside those dates even if they are
selected by another means. But files that fall within the accept-
able range still must be selected by some other means before they
are included in the setup. The special exclusions override all
other selection methods.

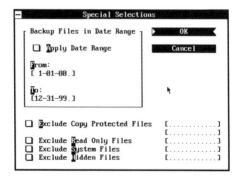

Figure 9.3.   *The items in the Special Selections dialog box identify
files to be excluded from the backup even if they are selected by some
other means.*

In the Select Backup Files dialog box (the DOS version), a check
mark identifies files that will be backed up. A dot indicates files
that are nominally selected for backup but currently are excluded
because their archive attributes are off (for an incremental or
differential backup) or because of the special exclusions.

Tip: For a printout of your entire setup, including backup options, restore options, compare options, and include and exclude statements, choose the File Print command.

Undoing File Selections

It is not always easy to undo file selections. You can review and edit the include and exclude list by choosing the Edit Include/ Exclude List button from the Include Files or the Exclude Files dialog box. (Both dialog boxes access the same list.) Once in the list, you can delete statements, switch them between include and exclude, revise the path or filespec, and so on.

If you select a whole drive for backup by selecting the drive name in the Backup From box, MSBACKUP generates an include statement for *.* on that drive. If you then deselect the drive, MSBACKUP changes the statement to an exclude statement so that none of the files on the drive are selected. You can delete the include and exclude statement from the list to return the drive to its normal status.

If you hand-select or deselect some directories or files and change your mind, there is no way to return individual files or directories to the control of the include and exclude list. You can undo all your manual selections and deselections by deleting the file named *setup*.SLT. All your manual selections are stored in this file, which works with the *setup*.SET file, where the rest of the setup is recorded, including the include and exclude list and the special exclusions. The SET file is an ASCII text file and can be edited, but the SLT file is not. The only way you can get rid of manual selections/deselections is to delete the SLT file.

Tip: The SET file contains some interesting information, such as the last backup using this setup, the last full backup using this setup, and so on.

To share your setup with other members of your workgroup, just copy the SET file to their hard drives. Don't copy the SLT file unless you also want to establish the same set of hand-selected and deselected directories and files on their computers.

Managing Backup Setups

By default, MSBACKUP stores all setup files in the same directory as the MSBACKUP program file. If you have several people using your computer, you may want to separate their backup setups so that people see only their own. Just create the desired directories and place the SET and SLT files in them. When you start up MSBACKUP, you can avoid the default setup file by including the desired setup name, including the path, in the command. The following command, for example, starts MSBACKUP with the WP setup from C:\DOS\JUDIDATA:

```
MSBACKUP C:\DOS\JUDIDATA\WP
```

Now that C:\DOS\JUDIDATA is the active directory for the setup, the commands on the File menu, such as Open Setup and Save Setup As, access this directory as the default directory.

Managing Backup Catalogs

Each time you make a backup, MSBACKUP records on your hard drive and on the backup disk or tape a catalog specific to that backup. It concocts a generic name for the catalog consisting of the drives that were backed up, the date, and the backup type. The catalog name CC41215A.DIF, for example, indicates a differential backup of drives C through C made in 1994 on 12/15. (The A indicates that this is the first CC41215*x*.DIF catalog made on 12/15/94.) This catalog lists the entire directory tree of the backed up drive(s) along with the directory entry of each file that was backed up.

Tip: The Restore function asks for disks by their catalog names, as in "disk #3 of CC41215A.DIF." If you forget to write the catalog names on the disk labels and are not sure which disk is which, you

can find out from the internal labels. MSBACKUP
assigns a volume label of *setup.typ*, as in
WPDAILY.DIF, and a file name of *catalog.nnn*, as
in CC41215A.003. (MSBACKUP concatenates all
backed up data into one file on the backup disk.)

MSBACKUP also maintains a master catalog for each of your
setups, named *setup*.CAT. The master catalog simply lists the
catalog names of the most recent full backup for that setup along
with the most recent differential backup or all the incremental
backups after the last full backup. In other words, the master
catalog identifies the entire set of backup catalogs you need to
fully restore the latest version of all files in that setup.

If you ask it to, MSBACKUP deletes old catalogs from your hard
drive as you create new ones so that only the current catalogs are
maintained. When you do a full backup, all previous individual
catalogs for that setup are deleted and all former catalog entries
in the master catalog are eliminated. When you do a differential
backup, MSBACKUP deletes all former differential catalogs for
that setup and removes their entries from the master catalog. No
catalogs are eliminated when you do an incremental backup. If
you want DOS to automatically eliminate old catalogs, deselect
the Keep Old Backup Catalogs option.

When a catalog is eliminated from the hard disk, it is a little
harder to access the files from that backup set. You have to
retrieve the catalog from the backup disks or tape before you can
restore any files. If you have plenty of hard disk space and you
think you will be accessing old backups frequently, consider
selecting the Keep Old Backup Catalogs option. When this
option is turned on, MSBACKUP does not eliminate old
catalogs from the hard drive or the master catalogs. You must
eliminate them yourself when you no longer need them.

By default, MSBACKUP stores all catalogs in the same directory
as its program file. You may want to specify a different directory
if you are on a network or if you have several users on your
system. Set the MSDOSDATA environment variable to tell
MSBACKUP where to store and retrieve catalogs. If your
CONFIG.SYS file is set up with configuration blocks for
different users, you can set a different value for MSDOSDATA
for each user.

Note: Chapter 6 explains how to set up multiple configuration blocks in CONFIG.SYS.

Suppose that your CONFIG.SYS file establishes configuration blocks for four users; your AUTOEXEC.BAT file uses the CONFIG variable to set up programs and environment variables for the four users. You might include commands like this in AUTOEXEC.BAT:

```
:JUDI
SET MSDOSDATA=C:\DOS\JUDIDATA
...

:DAVIDA
SET MSDOSDATA=C:\DOS\DAVIDATA
...

and so on
```

Deciding which Catalog to Open

With MSBACKUP, restoring files is often a simple matter of opening the desired catalog, selecting the file(s) you want, and choosing the Start Restore button. But which catalog do you open?

When you open an individual backup catalog, only the files in that catalog are listed for restoration. But when you open a master catalog, MSBACKUP shows the latest version of each recorded file (see fig. 9.4). A plus sign next to a file entry indicates that earlier versions are available in the same master catalog. When you select files for restoration, MSBACKUP tells you which disks to insert from which backup sets. Most of the time the master catalog is the best one to open because it identifies the latest versions of all files but also gives you access to earlier versions if you want them.

If you want to restore an earlier version of a file, highlight its entry and choose the Version button. A list of all versions available in the catalog appears, and you can select the version you want. That version replaces the default version in the file list.

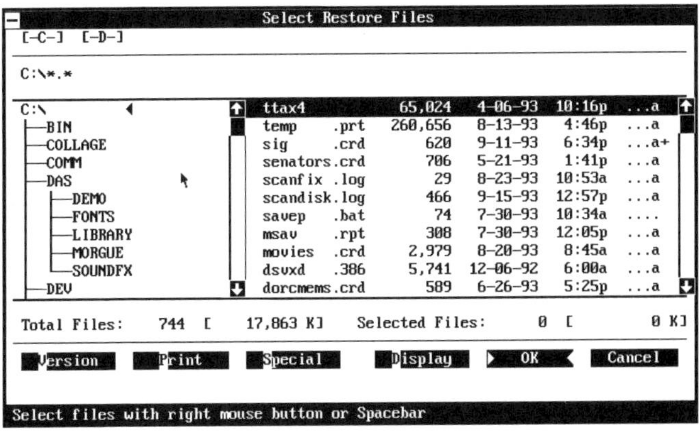

```
┌─────────────────────────────────────────────────────────────┐
│ ─                  Select Restore Files                      │
│ [-C-] [-D-]                                                  │
│ ─────────────────────────────────────────────────────────── │
│ C:\*.*                                                       │
│ ─────────────────────────────────────────────────────────── │
│ C:\         ◀  ↑  ttax4         65,024  4-06-93  10:16p ...a ↑│
│ ├─BIN          ▓  temp    .prt 260,656  8-13-93   4:46p ...a │
│ ├─COLLAGE      ▓  sig     .crd     628  9-11-93   6:34p ...a+│
│ ├─COMM            senators.crd     786  5-21-93   1:41p ...a │
│ ├─DAS       ▸     scanfix .log      29  8-23-93  10:53a ...a │
│ │ ├─DEMO          scandisk.log     466  9-15-93  12:57p ...a │
│ │ ├─FONTS         savep   .bat      74  7-30-93  10:34a .... │
│ │ ├─LIBRARY       msav    .rpt     308  7-30-93  12:05p ...a │
│ │ ├─MORGUE        movies  .crd   2,979  8-20-93   8:45a ...a │
│ │ └─SOUNDFX       dsvxd   .386   5,741 12-06-92   6:00a ...a │
│ ├─DEV       ▓     dorcmems.crd     589  6-26-93   5:25p ...a ▓│
│ ─────────────────────────────────────────────────────────── │
│ Total Files:  744 [  17,863 K]  Selected Files:  0 [  0 K]  │
│ ─────────────────────────────────────────────────────────── │
│ █ersion   █rint   █pecial   █isplay  ▶ OK ◀   Cancel        │
│ ─────────────────────────────────────────────────────────── │
│ Select files with right mouse button or Spacebar            │
└─────────────────────────────────────────────────────────────┘
```

Figure 9.4. *The Select Restore Files dialog box opens when you choose Select Files in the Restore window.*

Selecting the Best Restore Options

The best Restore options depend on what you are trying to accomplish. In all cases, use Verify Restore Data to guarantee the accuracy of the restored file.

If you are restoring a complete hard disk from scratch, you will not need Prompt Before Creating Directories, Prompt Before Creating Files, or Prompt Before Overwriting Existing Files. But you may want Restore Empty Directories so that MSBACKUP recreates the old directory structure even if some directories contain no files. This ensures that your applications' scratchpad directories are created.

If, instead, you are just replacing some files you deleted, you may want to use Prompt Before Overwriting Existing Files to make sure that you do not accidentally overwrite a newer version of a file with an older version. You will not need Restore Empty Directories or Prompt Before Creating Files in this case.

If you are replacing an existing file with an earlier version, do not use Prompt Before Overwriting Existing Files. You also do not need Restore Empty Directories or Prompt Before Creating Directories. You may want to use Prompt Before Creating Files to make sure that the file you select overwrites an existing one.

Restoring after a Crash

Suppose that your computer dies and you have to get a new one. After formatting the hard drive and installing DOS so that MSBACKUP is available, you can restore the latest versions of all your files from the backups. In this case, you will not have any catalogs available on the hard drive, so you must retrieve them one at a time from the backup disks.

Start with your last full backup. Insert the last disk of the set and choose the Catalog button in the Restore window. You see the select catalog dialog box. (see fig. 9.5). Choose the Retrieve button, which asks MSBACKUP to retrieve the catalog from the backup disk itself. (The catalog is always stored on the last disk in the set.) Choose the correct floppy drive and choose the OK button.

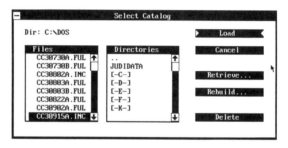

Figure 9.5.   *The Select Catalog dialog box enables you to open a catalog that is already present on the hard drive, or to retrieve or rebuild one from the backup disks.*

When MSBACKUP finishes retrieving the catalog, it adds the catalog name to the list in the dialog box and highlights it. All you have to do is choose Load to return to the Restore window with the retrieved catalog open and ready to use. To completely restore the backed up directory structure along with all its files, select the drive name(s) in the Restore Files box and choose Start Restore. MSBACKUP tells you which disks to insert.

If you make differential backups in between full backups, you should have the last differential backup that you made after your last full backup (if any). Repeat the process of retrieving the catalog from that backup, selecting the drive(s), and choosing Start Restore.

If you make incremental backups in between full backups, start with the first incremental backup that you made after the last full backup. Retrieve its catalog and restore everything from it. Keep restoring the incremental backups in chronological order until

they are all restored. It is important to do them in chronological
order so that newer versions of files overwrite older versions.

Restoring an Old File

Suppose that you want to restore a file that you deleted a year
ago. If you do not keep old catalogs on your hard drive, you will
have to retrieve the catalog from the backup disks. If you know
which backup set the file is in, retrieve the catalog from that set,
select the file, and choose Start Restore.

But what if you do not know which backup set contains the
correct version of the file you want? You will have to retrieve and
examine catalogs until you find it. After you finish this process,
you may reconsider keeping your old backup catalogs on the
hard drive.

Using MSBACKUP to Transfer Files to Another Computer

Suppose that you want to transfer a large set of data to another
computer. It may be one very large file—larger than one disk—
or it may be a large group of files. The best way is to link the two
computers via a network, teleprocessing, INTERLNK, or some
other means and transmit the data from one to the other. If you
cannot link them by any means, you must use disks or tape as an
intermediary.

If you are using disks or teleprocessing, MSBACKUP can
compress the data so that you have a lot less to ship. In the case
of a very large file that you need to transfer by disk,
MSBACKUP may be the only way to accomplish the task,
because it will split a file over two or more disks. No other DOS
utility will do that.

Prepare the files by backing them up using the compression
option. You also may use the verification and error-correction
options for safety's sake. If you plan to transmit the files via
telecommunication, back them up to a hard disk directory rather
than disk. Because reading and writing hard disk data is so much
faster, the files will take less time to back up, and a hard disk file
takes less time to transmit.

Warning: If you use a full or incremental backup to make the copies, the original files' archive attributes will be turned off, which could interfere with your regular backup cycle. Be sure to use a differential backup.

When you back up to a hard drive directory, MSBACKUP does not store the backup file in the indicated directory. Instead, it creates a subdirectory named for the setup and a subdirectory under that named for the catalog. MSBACKUP stores the backup file in that third-level directory. That is, if you back up to C:\TEMP, look for files named something like C:\TEMP\DAILYSET\CC31215A.FUL\CC31215A.001 (the backed up data) and C:\DOS\CC31215A.FUL (the catalog). Transmit both files and the recipient can load the catalog without retrieving it.

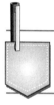

Note: If you transmit backed up files by floppy disk, the recipient must retrieve the catalog from the disk before restoring the files.

On the target computer, if you do not want to install the original computer's directory structure, do not select all the files by selecting the drive name(s) in the Restore Files box. If you want to restore the files to the same directory paths that they came from, choose Select Files to open the Select Restore Files dialog box, and then manually select each directory that contains files to be restored.

If you don't want to restore the files to the same directory paths, choose the Restore To button to open the dialog box shown in figure 9.6. If only the drive name is different but you want to restore to the original directory path names on that drive, choose Other Drives. MSBACKUP asks for the name(s) of the target drive(s).

To restore to different directory paths, whether or not the drive names are different, choose Other Directories. For each original directory, MSBACKUP gives you a chance to enter the name of the target drive and directory.

Figure 9.6. *Use the Restore To dialog box to restore files to a different drive or directory structure than they came from.*

Restoring without a Catalog

In some cases, you may have to restore files from a backup set that has been partially damaged and the catalog on the last disk is missing or destroyed. In that case, you can ask MSBACKUP to rebuild as much of the catalog as possible by reading through the backup disks. Choose the Rebuild button in the Select Catalog dialog box and follow the directions on-screen. You probably will not be able to restore all your files in this case, but maybe you can find the ones you need.

Comparing Backup Files

MSBACKUP's Compare function is nearly identical to its Restore function except that, instead of restoring the selected files, it compares them to the current disk version and warns you if the files are different or if they are missing from the disk. If any differences are found, you must decide on your own what to do next. In some cases, making new backups is the appropriate action. In others, restoring the files from their backups makes more sense.

When should you use the Compare feature? Some people use it immediately after backing up to make doubly sure that the backed up files are accurate. (The Verify option is a better choice, but some people use both.) You also can use Compare to find out whether a file has changed since its last backup. Compare also can tell you which files are missing from the hard drive; you may want to restore some or all of them.

Compare is also a good method to compare files on two different computers when you cannot link them up by any means. Follow the same procedure you would follow to transmit the files to the other computer, but instead of restoring the files on the target computer, use the Compare function to compare them.

Reconfiguring
MSBACKUP

MSBACKUP forces you to configure your hardware before making your first backup. The configuration tests make sure that MSBACKUP works accurately with your hardware as well as the terminate-and-stay-resident programs (TSRs) you usually have running in the background. If you make any changes to your hardware or your TSR setup, MSBACKUP probably will sense the changes and force you to reconfigure. If not, you should choose the Configure option and identify the new configuration. Be sure to rerun the compatibility test if you change the disk drives or any TSRs. Don't forget to choose the Save button at the end to save the new configuration.

10

Working with Microsoft AntiVirus

Yes, you do have to worry about viruses. They are rare, but they can be deadly. Viruses enter your system when you communicate with the outside world, either by linking your computer with another one via a network or telecommunications (or INTERLNK), or by inserting into your system a floppy disk that came from somewhere else. Once in your system, a virus takes up residence, usually in a program file or your boot sector. It also attempts to spread itself throughout your system and to other systems that you communicate with. The virus may not do anything else to your system, and what it does may or may not be harmful.

There are two primary ways to diagnose viruses. One is to *scan* your disks looking for telltale signs of a virus. Microsoft's antivirus programs can recognize more than 1,000 known viruses by unique sections of code they contain, called their *signatures*. An antivirus program also can spot unknown viruses, for which it has no signatures, by detecting that a program file or the boot record has changed since the last virus scan. The other primary method is to monitor all system activity for suspicious behavior, such as an attempt to change a program file or the boot sector, or an attempt to reformat the hard disk.

Microsoft's antivirus programs include both kinds of virus detection system. MSAV (and its Windows counterpart, MWAV) is a virus scanner. It can detect known and unknown viruses on a disk drive and in memory. In many cases, it can clean the virus; that is, it can remove the virus from the host file without damaging the host. In other cases, you must delete the host file and restore it from its backup. VSAFE is a virus monitor. It looks for eight specific symptoms of virus activity, intercepts them, and lets you decide whether to proceed or block them.

Can you afford to take the chance? Most power users feel that they cannot. It doesn't take more than a couple of minutes a day to scan for viruses, and they feel the time is well spent. A virus monitor can slow down your system slightly and takes up room in memory, but again, it is worth the extra resources to protect your data.

Deciding which Method to Use

Should you scan, or monitor, or both? In general, monitoring provides better protection because it prevents damage by viruses that could slip past the scanner. But complete monitoring interferes with every write to disk until you OK it, and you will find that annoying and counterproductive. A better compromise is to scan memory and your hard drive(s) each time you boot, and then monitor only the most suspicious activities, such as reformatting the hard disk. Also scan any floppies that have come from another computer. A new type of unknown virus could function in this environment, but the probability is low. And if you keep your virus definitions up to date, the probability becomes negligible.

Selecting the Best MSAV Options

MSAV runs in batch mode or interactive mode, but many of its options can be set only in interactive mode. The first time you run MSAV, run it in interactive mode so that you can set the options. After they have been saved in MSAV.INI, the same options are selected whether you use batch or interactive mode.

Note: If the default MSAV configuration is not compatible with your monitor or mouse, look up MSAV in DOS's on-screen Help system for a list of switches that control the hardware configuration.

Enter the command **MSAV** with no parameters or switches to start it up in interactive mode. Then click the Options button to display the dialog box shown in figure 10.1. The best options for you depend on what you want to accomplish.

Figure 10.1. *The Options Setting dialog box enables you to select options for MSAV's scanning process; MWAV offers similar options.*

Scanning for Unknown Viruses

Unknown viruses are usually the newest viruses and are more likely to be "going around" than the older, known viruses. Scanning for unknown viruses takes only a few seconds more, so you may as well take the extra precaution. You need the Verify Integrity option and the Create New Checksums option to scan for unknown viruses.

Note: MSAV always scans memory for viruses the first time you run a scan after starting MSAV.

Microsoft's antivirus programs diagnose unknown viruses by looking for any changes in program files. A change could indicate that a virus has invaded and taken up residence in the file. The first time you run a scan on a drive, Create New Checksums causes MSAV to create in each directory a file called CHKLIST.MS. The file contains control information, called *checksums*, for each program file in the directory. The checksums are so accurate that, if even one byte in a program file changes, the checksum changes and MSAV can detect that the program file has been altered.

On subsequent runs, the Verify Integrity option causes MSAV to recompute the checksums and compare them to CHKLIST.MS. Verify Integrity reports any differences it finds as suspected unknown viruses.

Also on subsequent runs, the Create New Checksums option causes MSAV to add to CHKLIST.MS checksums for any new programs that have been added to the drive since the last run.

It is not necessary to create checksums on floppy disks unless you use the same floppies all the time. If you often boot from a floppy or run a particular program from a floppy, it makes sense to protect that disk by scanning it with Create new Checksums, Verify Integrity, and Create Checksums on Floppy (you need all three options).

Controlling How MSAV Handles Viruses

During an interactive scan, the Prompt While Detect option causes MSAV to display a dialog box for each known or unknown virus it finds. The dialog box enables you to decide how to handle the suspected virus. If Prompt While Detect is disabled, MSAV's action depends on how you started the scan. If you started the scan with the Clean button or switch, MSAV does the best it can to handle the virus on its own. If it is a known virus that can be removed without damaging the host file, MSAV removes (cleans) it. Otherwise, MSAV makes note of the virus and moves on. For batch scans and interactive scans in which you did not use the Clean button or switch, MSAV simply makes note of the virus.

Note: To start a cleaning operation from the command prompt, include the /c switch with the MSAV command. To access the MSAV dialog box, press the Detect to Clean button or press F5. To detect without cleaning, omit the /c switch or press Detect (F4).

At the end of the scan, MSAV displays a summary showing the number of drives scanned, the number of files scanned, the number of viruses detected, the number cleaned, and so on. But you do not get any details on what files were suspect or what viruses were cleaned.

The Create Report option causes MSAV to create a more detailed report showing names of viruses and names of suspect files. If you run MSAV without Prompt While Detect, you need this report to find out details when viruses are suspected. MSAV stores the report in MSAV.RPT in the root directory of the scanned drive. It is an ASCII text file, so you can examine it with EDIT or print it.

If you do not use Prompt While Detect or Create Report, and if the end-of-scan summary shows uncleaned known viruses or suspected unknown viruses, you need to rerun the scan using Prompt While Detect or Create Report to find out where the viruses are so that you can deal with them.

Scanning for Maximum Protection

A *stealth* virus is a virus that attempts to disguise itself so that no signature can be identified for it. It also attempts to invade its host without changing the file's checksums. MSAV can check for stealth viruses when you select the Anti-Stealth option. The scan takes just a few seconds longer, so it is a worthwhile option.

Normally, MSAV scans files with extensions EXE, COM, OVL, OVR, SYS, BIN, APP, and CMD—the files most likely to be infected by viruses. If you select Check All Files, MSAV scans all files for known viruses, which takes quite a bit of extra time. Most people leave this option off. If MSAV encounters a virus that is known to infect data files, it suggests that you rerun the scan with this option turned on. (This option does not affect the unknown virus options.)

Preserving Infected Files

You may run into a situation in which a virus invades your only copy of a file; that is, you cannot restore the file from a backup. You may want to make a backup of the infected file in case the virus cannot be cleaned or the cleaning does not work. You can preserve infected files by turning on the Create Backup option. MSAV makes a copy of each infected file, assigning the VIR extension, before attempting to clean the virus. If the virus cannot be cleaned, you can save the VIR file until you can deal with the virus. Your next antivirus upgrade may include the information necessary to clean the virus. (See "Keeping your Virus Definitions Up to Date" later in this chapter.) Be sure to

delete all VIR files after their originals are cleaned successfully or
you can restore the originals from their backups. If you need to
keep a VIR file, move it to a floppy disk.

Running MSAV from AUTOEXEC.BAT

If you are going to scan your hard drive every time you boot, you
probably want to do it without opening the MSAV window.
When you add the /P switch to the MSAV command in
AUTOEXEC.BAT, MSAV runs automatically, displaying only
copyright messages, progress messages, and the summary report
at the end.

If you use the /N switch instead, the progress messages and end-
of-scan report also are suppressed. The copyright message, the
word working, and the filespecs being scanned appear on-screen.
Exit code 86 indicates that a virus was detected or suspected.
If you use /N, you should check for exit code 86 using IF
ERRORLEVEL 86 after the scan and proceed accordingly.

The /N switch was designed so that an experienced user can set
up virus scanning in AUTOEXE.BAT for an inexperienced user.
If you store a file named MSAV.TXT in the same directory as
MSAV.EXE, it is displayed during the scan instead of the
working message. You can display any message you want to a
user from MSAV.TXT.

> **Note:** When you use /N or /P, the scan does not
> clean viruses unless you also include the /C (Clean)
> switch.

You also may want to use the /F and /R switches. /F suppresses
the filespec display. /R forces an MSAV.RPT report to be issued
whether or not the Create Report option is selected in
MSAV.INI.

In summary, the following command starts a batch mode scan,
suppresses all messages except the copyright messages and
MSAV.TXT, scans drive C, issues an MSAV.RPT report, and
cleans any viruses that it can. The next command handles the 86

exit code. The VSTOP.BAT program may set up a closed loop
that displays a message over and over again (in the same screen
position) telling the user not to use the computer and to call you:

```
MSAV C: /N /F /R /C
IF ERRORLEVEL 86 C:\BATCHES\VSTOP.BAT
```

Scanning Multiple Drives

When you start MSAV in interactive mode, you can scan only
one drive at a time. But you can scan multiple drives in one scan
by specifying the drives in the command that starts MSAV. You
can include one or more drive names in the command, or you
can use the /A switch (for all nonfloppy drives) or the /L switch
(for all nonnetwork drives). The following command starts
MSAV to scan drives C and D, generating an MSAV.RPT report
regardless of the setting of the Create Report option in
MSAV.INI:

```
MSAV C: D: /R
```

If you specify more than one drive in the command, you bypass
interactive mode. Without the /P or /N switch, the MSAV
window appears, but you cannot access it. The scan happens
automatically, and you cannot read the summary report at the
end because MSAV terminates too quickly.

Scanning Specific Directories and Files

You do not have to scan a complete drive. You can include a
path name in the MSAV command to scan just the branch
headed by that directory. Suppose that you have just upgraded to
Windows 3.1 and you want to upgrade all the appropriate
CHKLIST.MS files in that branch. The following command
scans just the branch headed by C:\WINDOWS:

```
MSAV C:\WINDOWS
```

You also can scan an individual file. Suppose that your You Bet
program is misbehaving and you want to see whether it has been
infected by a virus. The following command scans just the
YOUBET.EXE file:

```
MSAV C:\YOUBET\YOUBET.EXE
```

> **Note:** You cannot use a global filespec in the MSAV command, and you must specify an absolute path (starting at the root directory) to scan a directory.

Setting Up MSAV for Multiple Users

> **Note:** Chapter 9 explains how to set the MSDOSDATA environment variable and how it affects MSBACKUP.

If your system is configured for more than one user, you probably want different MSAV.INI and MSAV.TXT files for each user. When the MSDOSDATA environment variable is set, MSAV looks in the indicated directory for MSAV.INI and MSAV.TXT. If MSAV.INI does not exist in that directory, MSAV creates a new directory using its default options.

You can copy your MSAV setup to another user or another computer by copying the MSAV.INI file. Suppose that your system is set up for three users: Judi, Davida, and Greg. MSDOSDATA points to C:\JUDIDATA, C:\DAVIDATA, or C:\GREGDATA depending on which user option is selected in CONFIG.SYS. To make sure that all three users use the same MSAV options, which are not the default options, you should copy your MSAV.INI file to all three directories. If you do not, MSAV creates an MSAV.INI with its default options in each of these directories.

Keeping Your Virus Definitions Up to Date

It is extremely important to keep your virus signatures up to date so that you can detect and clean the most current viruses. Your DOS 6 documentation includes information on how to download virus signatures from the antivirus BBS and how to upgrade your MSAV program. If you have a modem, you should check the BBS at least once a month. When you download virus signatures, you also receive instructions on how to install them. The downloaded signatures give you the ability to detect, but not clean, the latest viruses. You have to upgrade MSAV to be able to clean the signatures.

Using VSAFE with Windows

If you use VSAFE with Windows, you must take a couple of extra steps. First, do not install or upgrade Windows with VSAFE running. Unload VSAFE with the command VSAFE /U before starting the installation program.

Second, when you start Windows, you must load a program called MWAVTSR.EXE so that VSAFE can pop its alert boxes onto the Windows screen. Either edit WIN.INI to add MWAVTSR.EXE to the line that says load= or add MWAVTSR.EXE to the Startup group.

Choosing the Best VSAFE Options

Note: Look up VSAFE in DOS's on-screen Help system for its syntax, notes, and examples.

VSAFE offers eight monitoring options to help you intercept virus-like behavior and decide what to do. Two of the options are actually scanning options:

- Option 4 scans executable program files as DOS loads them; if CHKLIST.MS data is available, it also checks for unknown viruses as well as known viruses. You do not need this option if you regularly scan with MSAV. Otherwise, it is an excellent option to turn on.

- Option 5 scans the boot sector of every disk that you insert for known viruses. You would be wise to keep this option on, as many viruses travel in the boot sectors of disks.

Several other options monitor for and intercept typical virus-like behavior. Most of these options take up so little processing time that you will not notice the difference until VSAFE actually intercepts something:

- Option 1 intercepts all attempts to format the hard disk. Keep this option on at all times.

- Option 2 intercepts any program attempting to establish memory residence. Many viruses take up residence in memory when you load their host program. If you load all your terminate-and-stay-resident programs (TSRs) from AUTOEXEC.BAT and load VSAFE last, you will not be annoyed by VSAFE intercepting all your other legitimate TSRs. After all your legitimate TSRs are loaded, if VSAFE warns you of a program attempting to establish memory residence, there is a good chance that it is a virus.

- Option 3 intercepts all attempts to write to disk. As mentioned before, you probably do not want to use this option because it seriously impedes all your work.

- Option 6 intercepts any attempt to write to the boot sector of the hard disk. Unless you are reformatting the hard disk or installing DOS, no program should attempt to do this. Keep this option on at all times.

- Option 7 intercepts any attempt to write to the boot sector of a floppy disk. As mentioned before, this is a common way for viruses to spread. Keep this option on at all times, but be prepared for a few extra steps when you try to format a floppy. (Do not forget that programs like MSBACKUP automatically format floppies.)

- Option 8 intercepts any attempt to modify an executable file. This helps to prevent a virus from invading a program file. But you may want to turn it off when upgrading a program or set of programs. (If you have a program that modifies its own program file, perhaps when you change options or the configuration, it will generate some VSAFE alert boxes. After a while, you will get used to the program and will feel free to ignore the VSAFE messages.)

Note: Press Alt-V to display a list of VSAFE options. When the list is displayed under DOS, you can toggle an option on or off by typing its number. Under Windows, check or uncheck the desired option.

Dealing with Viruses

When MSAV is in interactive mode and the Prompt While Detect option is selected, MSAV displays a dialog box for each possible virus it finds. VSAFE does the same. The dialog box explains what known virus has been found or what symptoms have been detected and gives you a choice of actions. For a known virus, the actions may include cleaning the virus, deleting the host file, stopping the scan, or ignoring the virus and continuing. If the Clean button is available, it is usually the best choice, because it removes the virus from the file without damaging the host. Otherwise, let MSAVE or VSAFE delete the file, and then reinstall it from the original program disks.

For an unknown virus, the options may include deleting the host file, stopping the scan, updating CHKLIST.MS, or ignoring the situation and continuing the scan. If you know that the change in the file is legitimate, update CHKLIST.MS. Otherwise, you are best off deleting the file and reinstalling it from the original program disks. You also can check the virus update BBS to download the latest virus signatures; perhaps your unknown virus is now a known virus.

Tip: If you discover a truly unknown virus in your system, let the folks at Microsoft know. They may want a copy of the file containing the virus so that they can begin the process of turning it into a known virus. Who knows? Maybe they will even name it after you.

When VSAFE reports a suspicious action such as reformatting the hard drive, the choices may be to block the action or to allow it to continue. Your best choice depends on whether you know that the action is legitimate. If you know that you are trying to reformat the hard disk, for example, let the action continue. Otherwise, block the action, reboot immediately, and scan memory and your hard drive for viruses.

Tip: Always reboot after detecting and handling a virus. Rebooting removes the virus from memory if it has managed to install itself there.

Finding Out More about Specific Viruses

Suppose that you hear that the AirCop virus is going around. Can your version of MSAV detect and clean it? Or suppose that MSAV detects the Stoned virus in your system. What does this virus do? Is it harmful? MSAV includes a list of all the known viruses and strains it can detect. Access the list by pressing F9 from the MSAV window. You can scroll through the list or type the name of a virus or strain to jump right to it. When the desired virus is highlighted, choose the Info button to read about it.

Redoing the CHKLIST.MS Files

When you delete or move a program file, MSAV does not remove its entry from CHKLIST.MS. Every so often, you may want to clean up your CHKLIST.MS files by deleting all the existing files and creating new ones. Press the F7 key from the MSAV window to delete all CHKLIST.MS files on the selected drive. Then run a new scan using the Create New Checksums option to establish the new CHKLIST.MS files.

11

Recovering Data

Many things can go wrong with disk data. But even when your hard disk dies or your computer is stolen, you will not lose one byte of data if you keep your backups up to date. Sometimes, unfortunately, you need to recover a file from a damaged disk because you have no valid backup. This chapter discusses some of the things that can go wrong with a disk and how to recover data when they do.

Storing Data with DOS

Recovering data often requires an understanding of DOS's filing system, which controls the storage and retrieval of data on disks. DOS allocates disk space to a file in *clusters*; a cluster is one or more sectors. (The number of sectors in a cluster depends on the size of the disk; the larger the disk, the larger the cluster.) The clusters are numbered in sequence starting with 2. DOS often refers to clusters as *allocation units.*

DOS keeps track of files via a combination of directories and the file allocation table (FAT). Each directory entry shows the name of the file, its size, the date and time it was last updated, its attributes, and its first cluster number. The FAT contains an entry for every cluster on the disk. Each entry contains the number of the next cluster in the file. That is, if a file is stored in clusters 10, 11, and 12, the directory entry points to cluster 10; cluster 10's FAT entry contains the number 11; and cluster 11's FAT entry contains the number 12. Cluster 12's FAT entry contains a special code meaning end of file. Thus, DOS locates all the clusters in a file by tracing along a *chain* of FAT entries.

Whenever you create or modify a file, DOS must update the directory and the FAT to show where the file is located. When you delete a file, DOS places a 0 in all its FAT entries; a 0 indicates that a cluster is available for reuse. (DOS does not actually delete the data in the cluster, which is why you may be able to recover it.)

Note: DOS actually maintains two FATs on most disks. The second FAT is used primarily to check and repair the first FAT.

It is easy to develop problems in the filing system. Perhaps you shut down the system or something hangs it up before it can finish updating the FAT. A file may be deleted in the directory, but its clusters are not all zeroed in the FAT. Or the file size may be increased in the directory, but the new sectors never get recorded in the FAT.

You know your disk has FAT problems when part of a file disappears or the wrong data appears in it, indicating that DOS accessed the wrong clusters when reading the file. If a program suddenly misbehaves or will not even load, but MSAV finds no indication of a virus, it could be that the clusters are mixed up in the FAT. Or you may see garbage in a directory listing, indicating that DOS is looking in the wrong cluster for the subdirectory.

If anything damages the directory structure or FAT, you may not be able to access your files. DOS provides programs to diagnose and fix a disk's filing system. For versions of DOS before 6.2, the CHKDSK (Check Disk) program diagnoses, and perhaps fixes, problems in a disk's filing system. DOS 6.2 provides SCANDISK, which can locate and deal with physical problems on the surface of the disk, as well as repair the filing system. This chapter covers both CHKDSK and SCANDISK.

Note: DOS 6.2 includes both CHKDSK and SCANDISK. Use SCANDISK instead of CHKDSK for diagnosing and repairing disk problems. It's a better program.

Diagnosing and Repairing Problems in the Filing System

Note: Look up CHKDSK and in DOS's on-screen Help system to see its syntax, notes, and examples. If you have DOS 6.2, also look up SCANDISK.

Both CHKDSK and SCANDISK analyze the FAT and report on problems. SCANDISK attempts to fix problems automatically unless you include the /CHECKONLY switch. CHKDSK does not attempt to fix problems unless you include the /F switch.

Handling Lost Clusters

A *lost cluster* is a nonzero FAT entry that can no longer be linked up with a directory entry. Either a FAT chain has accidentally been broken because of a bad entry somewhere in the FAT, or DOS was interrupted before it could finish deleting a file so that some of the clusters were not zeroed. In the former case, you should see other messages indicating a problem; when you fix that problem, the lost clusters should be cleared up. In the latter case, you may not see any symptoms at all until you run CHKDSK or SCANDISK, but the lost clusters could be taking up a great deal of hard disk space. When you ask CHKDSK or SCANDISK to delete the clusters, you recover that space.

Note: You should run CHKDSK or SCANDISK about once a month on your hard drive to check for and clean up lost clusters.

> **Warning:** Open files can look like lost clusters (or
> some other FAT error), so never run CHKDSK or
> SCANDISK from another program such as
> Windows or DOSSHELL. Always exit all applica-
> tions and shells and run CHKDSK or SCANDISK
> from a primary command prompt.

When CHKDSK discovers lost clusters in the FAT, it displays a
message something like this:

```
115 lost allocation units found in 31 chains
235520 bytes would be freed
```

If you started CHKDSK with the /F switch, the second line
looks like this:

```
Convert lost chains to files (Y/N)?
```

If you are missing some data and want to try to recover it, press
Y. CHKDSK creates 31 files, one for each chain, in the root
directory of the disk, named FILE0000.CHK through
FILE0030.CHK. You need to examine the files to see if they
contain your missing data. Delete the CHK files you do not
want.

If you are not missing any files, simply press N. CHKDSK zeros
the lost clusters, freeing that space for other purposes.

SCANDISK explains problems better than CHKDSK. When
SCANDISK discovers lost clusters, it displays a dialog box like
the one shown in figure 11.1. If the explanation there isn't clear
enough for you, click More Info for more complete information.
When you're ready to make a decision, click Save to save the lost
clusters as a file or Delete to delete them.

Saving Undo Information with SCANDISK

The first time in a session that SCANDISK fixes a problem, it
offers to record undo information for you (see fig. 11.2). If the
fix makes matters worse rather than better, you can use the undo
information to restore the disk to its former condition. To
record undo information, click the Drive A or Drive B button.
In general, it costs very little to record undo information, so you
may as well take the extra precaution. But if you decide not to,
click the Skip Undo button. If SCANDISK finds more

problems in the same session, it continues to record or skip undo information without asking.

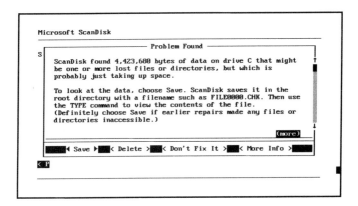

Figure 11.1. *SCANDISK explains detected problems in a dialog box similar to this.*

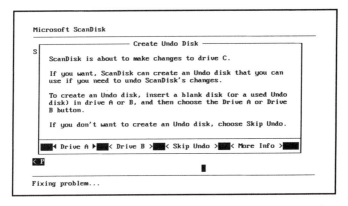

Figure 11.2. *SCANDISK offers to record undo information when it fixes a problem.*

To undo a fix, insert the undo disk into drive A or B and enter the following command, where *drive* is the name of the drive holding the undo disk, not the drive to be repaired:

SCANDISK /UNDO *drive*

Handling Cross-Linked Files

Two files are cross-linked when they use the same clusters. The first file may chain to clusters 10, 11, 12, 201, and 202, for example, and the second one to clusters 115, 116, 200, 201, and

202. SCANDISK reports that files are sharing the same clusters.
CHKDSK reports something like this:

```
C:\TRUSTEES\MARKHAM.DOC
  is cross-linked on allocation unit 201

C:\BATCHES\PASSES.BAT
  is cross-linked on allocation unit 201

C:\TRUSTEES\MARKHAM.DOC
  is cross-linked on allocation unit 202

C:\BATCHES\PASSES.BAT
  is cross-linked on allocation unit 202
```

In most cases of cross-linking, one file's chain is correct and the
other file's chain has been damaged. SCANDISK or CHKDSK
also may report lost clusters on the disk; some of them may be
the true end to the damaged file's chain.

> **Note:** Sometimes a file gets cross-linked on itself.
> It may chain to clusters 51, 52, 53, 54, 53, 54, 53,
> 54,..., for example. The file's true end probably
> appears as lost clusters.

SCANDISK attempts to fix cross-linked files by giving each file
its own copy of the shared clusters; however, this means that at
least one of the files ends up with the wrong data. CHKDSK
cannot fix cross-linkages because it has no idea which file is
correct and which is damaged, and it cannot tell which lost
clusters, if any, belong to the cross-linked files. Whether you
use SCANDISK or CHKDSK, your best action is to delete
the damaged files and restore them from their backups.

> **Note:** SCANDISK gives you two ways to find out
> the names of cross-linked files. You can select the
> More Info button when you see the cross-linked
> message, or you can examine the detailed report at
> the end of the SCANDISK session.

If you do not have valid backups, you can try to recover the data from the disk. First, let SCANDISK or CHKDSK convert lost clusters into files. Next, if you're using CHKDSK, you must exit the program and copy all the files involved. Some of the copies may contain the wrong clusters, but at least they will not be cross-linked. Then delete the cross-linked files. (If you're using SCANDISK, it performs this step for you.)

Next, you need to try to fix the damaged files. Unless they are executable program files, examine them using the applications that created them originally. In the example, you may use your word processor to examine MARKHAM.DOC and EDIT to examine PASSES.BAT. Figure out which file is damaged and delete the unwanted data from it. Then look in the CHK files to see whether you can find the real data. If so, open the file for editing again and insert the desired file(s) into it. Finally, delete any CHK files that you do not want.

Warning: Never try to repair a cross-linked program file. If you run a damaged program, it could do even more damage to your filing system. Simply delete the cross-linked file and reinstall the program. (If it is cross-linked to a data file, recover the data file using the techniques already discussed before deleting the program file.)

Handling Other Types of Errors

Other types of FAT errors are rare, but you may see one occasionally. Always restore damaged files from their backups if possible. If not possible, then let SCANDISK or CHKDSK fix the problem but be aware that the fix may not be perfect. In that case, recover lost clusters in case you need to edit and repair a file yourself. But your best solution, as always, is to restore damaged files from their backups.

An `invalid subdirectory entry` can be the most trouble-some problem. This message means that a subdirectory can no longer be linked with its parent. SCANDISK or CHKDSK usually repairs the linkage without any loss of data. But in some cases, CHKDSK cannot find the subdirectory's parent and

displays the message `Convert lost directory to file`
`(Y/N)`? Answer Y to this question because the resulting file is
a copy of the lost subdirectory. There is no way to turn it into a
subdirectory again, but at least you have a list of the files that
were in the damaged subdirectory. Restore the files from their
backups or, if that is not possible for some reason, try to find
them in the CHK files that were created from the lost clusters.
(This problem usually is accompanied by a large number of lost
clusters caused by all the abandoned files in the damaged
subdirectory.) If SCANDISK cannot reconnect a lost
subdirectory with its parent, it places the directory in the root
directory with a generic name (DIR00001). You can examine the
directory with DIR and rename it with MOVE.

An *invalid allocation unit* means that a file chains to a FAT entry
containing an invalid number. At that point, of course, the chain
is broken. SCANDISK or CHKDSK repairs the problem by
changing the invalid number to an end-of-file signal, cutting off
the true end of the file. Restore the file from its backup, or, if
that is not possible, try to fix the file yourself. If it is a program
file, delete it immediately. If it is a data file, open it for editing
and see whether you can recover its ending data from the CHK
files.

An *allocation error* means that the size in the directory entry does
not match the number of clusters in the chain. SCANDISK or
CHKDSK fixes this problem by adjusting the size in the directory entry. The file may lose or gain some data in the process.
When the repair program is done, delete and restore the file from
its backup. If that is not possible, you can try to fix the problem
yourself. If it is a program file, delete it immediately. If it is a
data file, open it for editing and delete the unwanted data at the
end or recover the missing data from the CHK files.

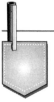

Note: When a cross-linkage causes a file to have a
different size than its directory entry shows,
SCANDISK finds and fixes the size error first.
Then it finds and fixes the cross-linkage. After
SCANDISK is done, your action is the same in
both cases: delete the damaged file and restore it
from its backup.

Unformatting Disks

If you accidentally reformat a floppy disk, you may not have backups of the data it contains. If you do not do an unconditional format, DOS's FORMAT program always stores unformatting information on the disk so that it is a simple matter to undo the formatting and recover the former data. Just enter an UNFORMAT command. If you do an unconditional format on the disk, the former data is overwritten by the low-level formatting and UNFORMAT cannot recover it.

Warning: If you added any data to the disk after reformatting it, unformatting may not be able to recover all the former files accurately.

Unformatting without an Unformatting File

It is possible to format a disk without recording unformatting information. If you use the /U and /Q switches together, for example, FORMAT does a quick format but does not store the unformatting information. You still can attempt to unformat such a disk, but the results will not be as satisfactory. UNFORMAT can search through the disk and recover subdirectories, and then undelete their files, but you will be left with several problems:

■ UNFORMAT cannot locate any files that were stored in the root directory. You may need a third-party undelete utility to seek out the unrecovered files in the free areas of the disk.

■ UNFORMAT can locate subdirectories of the root directory, but it has no way of knowing their original names. It assigns generic names to them: SUBDIR.1, SUBDIR.2, and so on.

■ UNFORMAT can find only the first fragment of a fragmented file. Again, a third-party undelete utility may be able to recover file fragments from the disk's free space.

Because most people rarely create subdirectories on a floppy disk, it may be that UNFORMAT cannot recover any data at all. You can run UNFORMAT with the /TEST switch to see what it can do without actually recovering anything. Use the /P switch to print the results.

Undeleting a Subdirectory

Another suggested use of UNFORMAT is to undelete a subdirectory. Because UNFORMAT can read the free space, recognize a subdirectory, and link it with its former parent, this seems like a good way to recover a deleted subdirectory. But UNFORMAT then goes on to recover all the files on the disk, whether or not they were in the deleted subdirectory, and in the process, it truncates all fragmented files. So here again, you are better off using a third-party utility to recover the deleted subdirectory. Both PC Tools and The Norton Utilities include undelete programs that can accurately undelete subdirectories and their files.

Undoing RECOVER

Microsoft also suggests using UNFORMAT to recover your directory structure if you accidentally destroy it with the RECOVER command (explained later in this chapter). But because of the limitations already mentioned, the recovery is less than satisfactory. The Norton Utilities includes a program called Recover from DOS's RECOVER that does a much better job.

Dealing with Disk Read and Write Errors

When you do an unconditional format on a disk, the formatting program tests the surface for reliability by writing, and then reading the entire disk. If the format program finds any bad spots, it marks them with a special code in the FAT so that DOS does not try to record any data there. At that point, the remainder of your disk surface should be totally reliable.

Sometimes sectors are damaged after formatting. Then you may begin to see Read Error and Write Error messages when you access certain files. DOS will not normally access any part of a file that encounters a read or write error, even though most of the sectors belonging to the file are perfectly fine. If this happens to you, try to access the file several times. If it still does not work, you may need to recover the file by some means.

If several new bad spots develop on your hard disk, you may wonder what is happening. It could be that your drive heads are crashing into the tracks when you shut down and you need to use a head-parking program before shutting down. Or your hard drive may be getting old and in need of replacement.

Using SCANDISK

After SCANDISK has checked and perhaps repaired a disk's filing information, it offers to scan the surface of the disk for physical flaws. If any flaws are found, SCANDISK moves as much data as possible away from the damaged area, and then marks the affected clusters as unusable (just as FORMAT does when it finds bad clusters). The rescued files may not be complete. Delete and restore them from their backups.

You should run SCANDISK on all your hard drives periodically to check for surface faults. (Use the /SURFACE switch to run the surface scan without being asked.) If you get any kind of a read error on a disk that prevents you from accessing one or more files, run SCANDISK's surface test to block out the damaged area. Then restore the damaged file from its backup.

Using DOS's RECOVER

DOS used to include a RECOVER program that would recover the good sectors from a file, move them to a safer location, and block out the bad sectors in the FAT. Unfortunately, if you entered the wrong RECOVER command, it blasted your entire directory structure, recovering every file on the drive into the root directory and assigning it a generic name. When it was done, the disk had no subdirectories and perhaps thousands of files in the root directory named FILE0000.REC, FILE0001.REC, and so on.

RECOVER had such a bad reputation that Microsoft finally eliminated it from DOS 6, and then added SCANDISK to DOS 6.2. However, if you upgraded to DOS 6.0 and have not yet stepped up to DOS 6.2, you may still have the RECOVER program. If so, you will have to decide for yourself if you want to try it. A power user should be able to do so safely. As long as you include a filespec with the RECOVER command, it recovers only the indicated file. The following command quite safely recovers the MADIRA.TXT file:

```
RECOVER C:\TEXTS\MADIRA.TXT
```

Note: You must use a single filespec. RECOVER reports `File not found` in response to a global filespec.

The situation to avoid is entering the RECOVER command with only a drive name. The following command destroys the directory structure of drive C. RECOVER displays the message shown in the example, but even then some people enter Y without realizing what is going to happen.

```
RECOVER C:
The entire drive will be reconstructed,
directory structures will be destroyed.
Are you sure (Y/N)?
```

If you have SCANDISK, you don't need RECOVER. Delete it from your DOS directory so that no one else decides to find out what the RECOVER.EXE file does.

Dealing with Sector Not Found Errors

You also may bump into occasional `Sector Not Found` errors on a disk. This happens when the disk's formatting is beginning to deteriorate. It is a good indication that the disk needs to be unconditionally reformatted or thrown away. In the meantime, you will not be able to access files with missing sectors.

This is another good time to reach for a third-party utility. Most of them include programs that can refresh a disk's sector information without destroying any data. DOS has no such program.

If you have to use DOS to refresh a floppy, back up as many files as possible, reformat the disk using the /U switch so that FORMAT redoes the sectors, and restore the files. For a hard disk, bring your backups up to date, if necessary, and then run a low-level formatting program on it. (You need an outside program for this; DOS does not include one.) Then repartition the disk with FDISK, reformat the partitions, and restore the data.

12

Making Full Use of the DOS Environment

DOS reserves a small area of conventional memory, called the *environment,* for its own variables. The environment contains such information as the current search path and the current prompt definition. You also can use the DOS environment to store information for your batch programs and applications.

Defining Environment Variables

You may want to define some environment variables of your own. You can control some DOS utilities by placing variables in the environment. The DIRCMD variable, for example, establishes default switches for the DIR command. The MSDOSDATA variable establishes a default directory for MSBACKUP and MSAV. You also may have other applications that look for variables in the environment. In fact, you can access environment variables from your own batch programs, as explained in Chapter 3.

Note: Look up SET in DOS's on-screen Help system to see its syntax, notes, and examples.

The following command creates an environment variable named MSDOSDATA with the value C:\USERS\JUDI:

```
SET MSDOSDATA=C:\USERS\JUDI
```

To change the value of a variable, simply redefine it with the new value. To delete a variable from the environment, define it with a null value. The following command deletes the MSDOSDATA variable:

```
SET MDDOSDATA=
```

DOS does not control the data you place in the environment. It simply stores whatever you tell it to. It is up to the programs that access the environment to make sense out of the information they seek.

Viewing the Environment

If you want to see what is in your environment, enter the SET command with no parameters, as shown in the following example:

```
C:\>SET

COMSPEC=C:\DOS\COMMAND.COM
PATH=C:\DOS;C:\WINWORD;C:\NDW;C:\WINDOWS
PROMPT=$P$G
TEMP=E:\
WINDIR=C:\WINDOWS
```

Expanding the Environment

The DOS default environment size is only 256 bytes, and you can fill that up rather quickly. The previous example, for example, takes up more than 100 bytes. If you try to define a new variable and receive the message Out of environment space, you have to delete something or increase the size of the environment.

Note: Look up COMMAND in DOS's on-screen Help system to see a list of switches that you can use when loading COMMAND.COM in the SHELL command.

You can establish a larger environment when you boot by including a SHELL command in CONFIG.SYS. Identify COMMAND.COM as the shell program and include the /E switch to define the environment. Be sure to include /P to make the shell permanent; otherwise you may hang up the system. The following command establishes COMMAND.COM as the shell and requests a 512-byte environment:

```
SHELL=C:\COMMAND.COM  /E:512  /P
```

The environment is placed in conventional memory, even if DOS is loaded high, so don't request more space than you actually need.

Working with a Secondary Environment

When you request a DOS command prompt from a shell such as DOS Shell or Windows or from an application such as WordStar, you get a *secondary* command environment, subordinate to the original, parent environment. Any environment changes you make are stored in the secondary environment only; they do not affect the parent environment. When you enter EXIT to return to the shell or application, the secondary environment is removed from memory and you go back to the parent environment. Any changes you made to environment variables, including the command prompt and the search path, are forgotten when the secondary environment is terminated.

You also can request a secondary environment directly from the primary command prompt with the COMMAND command. This actually loads a second copy of COMMAND.COM, complete with its own environment. You may want to do this to make temporary changes to the environment or to temporarily obtain a larger environment. Suppose that an application requires five environment variables and there is not enough room left to set them. The following command opens a secondary COMMAND.COM with 1K of environment space:

```
COMMMAND  /E:1024
```

The secondary command environment inherits all the parent environment's variables. Any changes you make to the environment are dropped when you enter **EXIT** to return to the primary command prompt.

Preserving Environment Variables

Suppose that you are creating a batch program that makes
temporary changes to the PATH, PROMPT, and TEMP
variables. The easiest way to preserve the original variables and
restore them again is to start a secondary environment, make the
changes, do whatever work the batch program is designed for,
and then EXIT back to the primary command environment. The
following commands show a skeleton of this routine (specific
command parameters are omitted):

```
REM The following command starts a secondary
➡ command environment
COMMAND
PATH ...
PROMPT ...
SET TEMP=...


REM The following commands do the processing
➡ for this program
..


REM The following command restores the primary
➡ command environment
EXIT
```

Creating an Empty Secondary Environment

Sometimes DOS needs to reload the transient portion of the
command interpreter after running a program. The COMSPEC
variable tells DOS where to find the command interpreter in
that situation. If there is no COMSPEC variable, DOS looks
in the root directory of the boot drive. If you are using
C:\COMMAND.COM as your command processor, you do
not need to specify a COMSPEC variable.

In the SHELL and COMMAND commands, you can specify a
path for the COMSPEC variable. The following command
indicates that the command processor is in the DOS directory
instead of the root directory:

```
SHELL=C:\DOS\COMMAND.COM C:\DOS\ /P
```

The path specified in the second parameter is the one that causes
DOS to set the COMSPEC variable. If it does not match the

path specified with the first parameter, DOS loads COMMAND.COM from one location but reloads it from another. Such disparity may or may not cause problems.

When you start a secondary command prompt, if the COMMAND command includes the COMSPEC path, DOS sets the specified COMSPEC variable in the new environment. It also provides a null search path for the secondary environment. Other than that, the new environment is empty. Even the PROMPT variable is missing, so DOS's default command prompt (C>) appears. In other words, when COMSPEC is specified, the secondary environment does not inherit the parent's environment. Suppose that you want to obtain a secondary command environment for a batch job with maximum room for your own variables. The following command starts a secondary environment with only a COMSPEC variable:

```
COMMAND C:\
```

When you EXIT to the primary command environment, the original variables are still there.

Redirecting the Output of a Batch Program

As mentioned in Chapter 3, you cannot redirect the output of a batch program. Redirection is ignored in the following command:

```
C:\BATCHES\LISTER.BAT > PRN
```

But the COMMAND command gives you a means to redirect batch output. You can start a secondary command prompt long enough to run one program, and you can redirect the output of that program, even if it is a batch program. The following command runs LISTER.BAT, redirecting the output to PRN:

```
COMMAND /C: C:\BATCHES\LISTER.BAT > PRN
```

When you use the /C parameter, COMMAND automatically exits the secondary environment as soon as the specified program terminates.

Interactively Executing Batch Programs

With DOS 6.2, you can execute a batch program on a line-by-line basis, just as you can with CONFIG.SYS and AUTOEXEC.BAT. The following command executes DRIVERS.BAT interactively:

```
COMMAND /Y /C C:\DRIVERS.BAT
```

For each line in DRIVERS.BAT, DOS displays this message:

```
command [Y/N]?
```

If you press Y, the command is executed. If you press N, that line is skipped and DOS goes on to the next line. When the program is finished, DOS exits the secondary environment.

13

Speeding Up Your Hard Disk

One major factor influencing the overall speed of your system is the access speed of your hard disk. Because your computer must access the hard disk so often, the faster its access time, the more work you get done. There are many things you can do to optimize your hard disk's access times.

Defragmenting Files

As you delete files, create new ones, expand some files, and shrink others, the free space on your drive gets divided into chunks located here and there instead of in one large area. When you create a new file, DOS may break it into several fragments to fit it into the available free space. When you expand a file, DOS may be forced to fragment it if the next clusters on the drive are already in use.

It takes longer to access a fragmented file than a contiguous one. After a while, your hard drive may have developed enough fragmentation to noticeably slow down the performance of your hard disk, and thus your entire system. Defragmenting your hard drive every so often can help keep your system running at its best. This process is often referred to as optimizing because it optimizes hard disk performance.

Preparing for DEFRAG

DOS's DEFRAG program defragments the files on a drive. DEFRAG works by rearranging the clusters on the drive. There are many things you should do before running it:

- Review your directories and delete any files that you do not need any more. Deleting them now means that DEFRAG does not have to waste time moving their clusters; it also gives DEFRAG more free space to work in.

- Run SCANDISK or CHKDSK with the /F switch if
  you're not using DOS 6.2 to fix any problems in the file
  allocation table (FAT) and directory tree and to free (or
  recover) lost clusters.

- Check for hidden and system files, which DEFRAG will
  not move. Files such as the DOS core files, IO.SYS, and
  MSDOS.SYS need to be in certain positions on the drive
  and shouldn't be moved. You may have other files that
  should not be moved because their copy-protection
  scheme requires them to always maintain the location
  where they were installed. In general, such files are
  assigned the hidden or system attributes. Make sure that
  any file that should not be moved has the hidden or
  system attribute. Consider removing hidden and system
  attributes from any files that can be moved safely.

- Unload or disable any TSR that may write to the drive
  during defragmentation. It is extremely important not to
  access a drive that DEFRAG is working on.

- Unload or disable any disk-caching program except
  SMARTDRV. DEFRAG knows how to inhibit
  SMARTDRV, but if you use an independent caching
  program, you must disable it before starting DEFRAG.

- Exit all programs (except TSRs), including Windows and
  DOS Shell. Never run DEFRAG with any files open or
  you could suffer serious data loss.

Identifying the Drive to Optimize

When you start DEFRAG, it runs a memory test to make sure
that it can move data around accurately. Then a dialog box asks
you to select the drive you want to optimize. DEFRAG analyzes
that drive and displays a map of its clusters as well as a recommended optimization method (see fig. 13.1).

Understanding the Drive Map

No matter how large the drive, DEFRAG always displays the
drive map in one screen. This means that each block on the map
may represent one cluster (for a double-density floppy) or dozens
of blocks. The Legend box in the lower right corner tells you
how many clusters are in each map block.

Figure 13.1. *DEFRAG displays a map of the selected drive and a recommended optimization method; the legend in the lower right corner helps you interpret the map.*

The map symbols indicate the most important clusters in the block, not necessarily the entire block. Blocks marked with X contain at least one cluster that cannot be moved because of a hidden or system file; they also may have some used clusters and some unused clusters. Blocks marked as used may have some unused clusters, but they do not have any unmovable or bad clusters. Blocks marked as unused are completely unused.

Tip: You can examine the entire map by choosing the Configure button to eliminate the Recommendation dialog box, and then clicking anywhere on the map or pressing Esc to remove the Optimize menu.

Selecting the Best Optimization Method

DEFRAG offers two optimization methods:

■ Full Optimization. This method moves all directories to the front of the drive so that DOS does not have to move the disk read/write heads so far to access them. Then it moves all files to follow the directories, defragmenting them as much as possible. It moves all free space to the end of the disk so that new files stored on the disk will not be fragmented. Full Optimization takes a lot more time than the other method, but it leaves your drive in tip-top condition. You may want to choose this method before installing a major new application on a drive so that the new files will not be fragmented.

■ Unfragment Files Only. This method defragments the files but does not move the directories to the beginning; it also may leave chunks of free space in the midst of the file area. It takes much less time than the other method, and the result is not quite as optimal. You should use Full Optimization if you have the patience to wait for it.

DEFRAG works at high speeds if possible, and can optimize a 120M hard drive full of data in just a few minutes on a 486. So the difference in time between the two methods is not all that significant.

If you want to use the recommended method, choose the Optimize button. Otherwise, choose the Configure button so that you can set up the desired optimization task.

Sorting Directories

DEFRAG also sorts directories if you ask it to. Sorting the directories affects only the order of the directory entries, not the files themselves. A sorted directory makes a difference in the order that files are processed by commands with global filespecs. It also makes a nicer presentation when you ship a set of files to a colleague or customer. To sort your directories, choose Optimize File Sort and select the desired sort order (see fig. 13.2). Both optimization methods sort the directories while optimizing if you have selected a sort order other than Unsorted.

After you select the drive, the optimization method, and perhaps the sort order, choose Optimize Begin Optimization (or press Alt+B) to start optimizing. DEFRAG displays its progress on the drive map and in the Status box as it works.

Tip: After about 10 percent of the optimization has been completed, you can use the Elapsed Time readout to estimate how much longer the optimization will take.

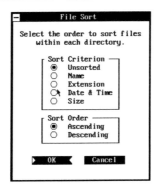

Figure 13.2. *Selecting a sort order in this dialog box causes DEFRAG to sort directories while it optimizes.*

Warning: Always reboot after DEFRAG to clear any caches and buffers of old FAT and directory data. Otherwise, you could lose some data on the optimized drive. If you include the /B switch on the command that starts DEFRAG, it reboots automatically after the optimization is finished.

Deciding when to Optimize

When you consider all the preparatory steps, DEFRAG can be a pain in the neck. Fortunately, you do not need to run it very often. Depending on the size of your hard disk, the amount of free space, and the number of files you have deleted, you may need to run it once a week, once a month, bimonthly, or less.

You can start DEFRAG and take a look at the percentage of fragmentation in the Recommendation window to decide whether it is time to optimize. Also look at the drive map to see the relationship between used and free blocks. If you decide that you do want to optimize, exit DEFRAG and prepare the drive before starting the optimization.

Automating DEFRAG

> **Note:** Look up DEFRAG in DOS's on-screen Help system to see the parameters that can be used in the DEFRAG command line.

You can run DEFRAG in batch mode by including all the necessary information on the DEFRAG command. Basically, DEFRAG needs to know the drive and the optimization method. The following command, for example, defragments drive D using Full Optimization in batch mode. (The DEFRAG window still opens so that you can watch the defragmentation process on the drive map.)

```
DEFRAG D: /F
```

You also can specify the directory sort order, /B to boot automatically after optimizing, and /SKIPHIGH to load DEFRAG into conventional memory.

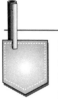

> **Note:** DOS's Help system indicates that you cannot specify a sort order with the /U switch (for Unfragment Files Only), but that is not true. Both optimization methods sort directory entries if requested.

Optimizing Hidden Files

You can include an /H switch on the DEFRAG command to permit DEFRAG to optimize hidden files (but not system files). If you do this, be sure that all files that should not be moved have the system attribute.

Defragmenting DoubleSpace Drives

Defragmentation usually is not a problem in compressed volumes, so you don't need to defragment them on a regular basis. But if you're running out of space on the drive or if you want to make the drive smaller, use the defragmenter with the /F switch to combine all the free space. In the first case, you could end up with more usable space on the drive. In the second case, you will have a larger space to remove from the drive.

For maximum effect, use DEFRAG on the compressed drive first; then use DoubleSpace's DEFRAG function on it. That is, first you enter a command such as DEFRAG *d:* /F. Then you enter a command such as DBLSPACE /DEFRAG *d:* /F.

Warning: When you defragment a host drive, be sure that all of DoubleSpace's files, including the CVF, have the same attributes they had when DoubleSpace originally created them: system, hidden, and read-only. If not, severe data loss could result.

Caching

Disk accesses are slow when compared to memory accesses, so you can speed up your system considerably by storing often used disk data in memory and accessing it from there. SMARTDRV is DOS's disk-caching program. It captures all disk data that you read and write and stores it in a memory buffer called a *cache.* If you read it again, it is read from the cache instead of the disk. When the cache is full, new data replaces the least used (not the oldest) data in the cache. After you have been using the cache for a while, it tends to hold your most active data, such as the root directory, the FAT, and the file you are working on.

Warning: Do not use two caching programs. If you already use a third-party caching system, you must choose between it and SMARTDRV. Double-caching can slow down your system and cause data loss.

When you read a file in sequential order, as when you are loading it, and the file is not fragmented, you read sector after sector in sequence. Whenever you read a sector from the disk, SMARTDRV actually reads several sectors into the cache on the assumption that those are the sectors you will want to read next. If so, SMARTDRV supplies them from the cache and you save the disk access time.

When you write data, SMARTDRV captures the written data in the cache. If you read the same data again, it is supplied from the cache.

If you want, SMARTDRV can delay writing to the disk for a short while so that you can read your next input data and continue processing. When you use the delayed writes feature, SMARTDRV writes the data when you are not occupied with reading. *Delayed writes* mean that your system does not have to wait for a write to be completed before it can continue working on the next task. It also means that if you write something several times in a short period of time, as in updating the FAT, only the final version is actually written to the disk.

Because there is some chance of losing delayed writes if the system goes down, SMARTDRV never delays written data for more than five seconds. It also writes delayed data if you press Ctrl+Alt+Delete or if it needs room in the cache for other data. You also can force SMARTDRV to write all delayed data with the command SMARTDRV /C. With DOS 6.2, SMARTDRV also flushes the cache automatically before returning to the command prompt, so you never need the SMARTDRV /C command.

Warning: If you use the delayed writes feature and haven't upgraded to DOS 6.2, be sure to enter the command **SMARTDRV /C** before shutting off the power to your computer. Otherwise, you could lose some data that you thought was written to the disk. This is especially important if you're using DoubleSpace with DOS 6.0. Forgetting to clear the SmartDrive buffers could result in extensive data loss on a compressed drive.

With versions of DOS before 6.2, SMARTDRV automatically write-caches hard drives; you have to specifically turn off write-caching if you don't want it. If you upgrade to version 6.2 from an earlier version, that situation is still true. But if you install DOS 6.2 from scratch, all write-caching is disabled by default. You have to specifically request write-caching, drive by drive, to turn it on.

Loading SMARTDRV

Note: Look up SMARTDRV in DOS's on-screen Help system to see its syntax, notes, and examples.

The simple command SMARTDRV loads SMARTDRV in its default state, but you may want more control over the size of the cache, which drives are cached, delayed writes, and so on. You do not need to specify LOADHIGH; SMARTDRV automatically loads into upper memory if it can.

Windows seizes control of the SMARTDRV cache when it starts, reducing the cache to give itself more workspace in memory. If you do not run Windows as your main user interface but start it only for specific applications, then you may want to specify a certain minimum size for the cache so that your most active cached data is not eliminated by Windows. The following command, for example, loads SMARTDRV.EXE, turns on read caching (only) for drive C, turns off all caching for the floppy drives, establishes a 3M cache when DOS is running, and establishes a minimum cache size of 1M when Windows is running:

```
SMARTDRV C A- B- 3072 1024
```

Deciding on Double-Buffering

SMARTDRV includes one feature called double-buffering that must be loaded as a driver from CONFIG.SYS. You should not install SMARTDRV.EXE from CONFIG.SYS unless your hard drive requires double-buffering. After loading SMARTDRV from the command prompt, enter the command **SMARTDRV /S**. A report similar to the following results:

```
Microsoft SMARTDrive Disk Cache version 4.1
Copyright 1991,1993 Microsoft Corp.
```

```
Room for    256 elements of   8,192 bytes each
There have been  5,363,127 cache hits
    and   206,460 cache misses

Cache size:   2,097,152 bytes
Cache size while running Windows:   1,048,576 bytes


               Disk Caching Status
drive     read cache      write cache  buffering
 — — — — — — — — — — — — — — — — — — — — — —

  A:          yes             no          no
  B:          yes             no          no
  C:          yes             yes         no


For help, type "Smartdrv /?".
```

In the Disk Caching Status table near the end of this message, look at the third column. If any of the entries say "yes" or "—", you need double-buffering. In that case, in addition to starting up SMARTDRV as before, you load double-buffering with a DEVICE command in CONFIG.SYS as follows:

```
DEVICE=C:\SMARTDRV.EXE DOUBLE_BUFFER
```

Reading the Status Report

The SMARTDRV status report gives you other valuable information. If you loaded SMARTDRV using all default values, you may not know how big your cache is. You can find out from the report. In the example, the basic cache size is 2M and the minimum size with Windows is 1M.

Understanding Cache Elements

SMARTDRV stores data in elements in much the same way that your hardware stores data in sectors. SMARTDRV reads and writes one element at a time. When you request one sector's worth of data that is not already in the cache, SMARTDRV actually reads a whole element. When you read the next sector, it is all ready for you. In general, large elements mean that SMARTDRV has to read from and write to the disk less often, maximizing the benefit of data caching. That is why the default element size is SMARTDRV's maximum element size of 8,192 bytes.

You can request a smaller element size, but in most systems there is very little reason to do so. If your work consists almost entirely of updating a database in random order so that you are not reading sectors in sequence, then try making the element size smaller. If the database record size is 272 bytes, for example, try the smallest element size (1,024 bytes). The hit-to-miss ratio shown in the status report, which is explained in the next section, can help you evaluate the effect.

If you use the /E parameter to request a smaller element size, also specify the cache size parameters and put the /E parameter first. If you omit the cache size parameters or put /E after them, SMARTDRV calculates the number of elements based on the default element size of 8,192 bytes, and then reduces the cache size to hold just that number of elements. If you request a 2M cache with or without Windows, for example, SMARTDRV calculates that there should be 256 elements of 8,192 bytes each. If it then encounters an /E parameter requesting an element size of 1,024 bytes, it adjusts the cache size to 256K, enough to hold 256 elements of 1,024 bytes each. The following command results in a 256K cache with 256 elements:

```
SMARTDRV 2048 2048 /E:1024
```

The following command results in a 2M cache with 2,048 elements:

```
SMARTDRV /E:1024 2048 2048
```

Calculating the Hit Rate

The SMARTDRV status report also reports the number of cache hits and misses. A *hit* means that SMARTDRV was able to read data from or update it in the cache, avoiding a disk access. A *miss* means that SMARTDRV had to read from or write to disk. The system in the example had been in use for a long time; there were more than 5 million hits and only 2,000 misses for a 25:1 ratio. SMARTDRV is capturing 96 percent of this system's disk accesses!

You can use the hit-and-miss data to evaluate the effectiveness of SMARTDRV in your system. If you are experimenting with different cache and element sizes, do about an hour's worth of your normal work using a SMARTDRV configuration, and then calculate the percentage of hits. By the end of a day or so, you should be able to identify the best configuration for your system.

Using SMARTMON

If you have Windows, DOS's SMARTMON program can help you evaluate your SMARTDRV performance. Figure 13.3 shows the SmartDrive Monitor window. In the Cache Memory group at the upper left, you can see the size of the cache with and without Windows. The Commit button forces SMARTDRV to write all delayed data. The Reset button writes all delayed data and then clears the caches.

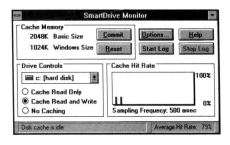

Figure 13.3.   *The SmartDrive Monitor window depicts your cache activity and enables you to adjust drive caching status.*

The Drive Controls group at the bottom left shows what caching is in effect for each of your drives. Select a drive in the drop-down list to see its current caching status. You also can change the status by selecting a different one.

The Cache Hit Rate provides a dynamic visual display of your cache activity. The graph is updated frequently to give a visual picture of your cache activity. The cache hit rate also is displayed as a percentage in the status bar at the bottom right. The message at the bottom left flips between `Disk cache is active` and `Disk cache is idle` as you work on tasks.

By default, the SMARTMON window stays on top of all your other windows, even when you are working in a maximized window, so that you can always see the effect of your work on the cache.

If you minimize the window, the minimized icon also stays on top of all other windows and shows the hit rate. SMARTMON continues to display the hit rate in the minimized icon. When it actually takes a sample, the hit rate appears in red on a color monitor. Otherwise, the average hit rate is displayed in the default text color.

Tip: If you do not like the SmartDrive Monitor window staying on top of your active window, pull down its control menu and deselect the Always On Top option.

The Options button opens a dialog box in which you can configure SMARTMON (see fig. 13.4). You can set the frequency at which SMARTMON samples the hit rate (Sampling Frequency) and the number of bars to display on the chart (Histogram Display Intervals). By default, SMARTMON samples the hit rate every 500 milliseconds (1/2 second) and shows 30 samples at a time. You can specify a sampling frequency between 50 and 10,000 milliseconds and display intervals between 3 and 100.

Figure 13.4. *The SmartDrive Monitor Options dialog box enables you to configure SMARTMON.*

SMARTMON logs your cache activity to a disk file if you want. This gives you a more permanent record of cache activity. To start logging, choose the Start Log button. By default, SMARTMON logs cache activity to a file named SMARTMON.LOG in the default directory. It logs for two hours (120 minutes) by default. You can stop logging earlier by selecting the Stop Log button. And you can configure logging to log to a different file and to stop automatically after so many minutes by selecting the Options button.

If you make changes to the disk-caching status, they will be forgotten the next time you boot unless you ask SMARTMON to record them in the batch file that contains your SMARTDRV command (AUTOEXEC.BAT by default). If you select Save

Setting in DOS Batch File, SMARTMON actually edits the
SMARTDRV command in the file indicated by File Name
with the appropriate drive switches.

Deciding on Cache Size

SMARTDRV always places the cache in extended memory, so
the bigger the better. Calculate how much extended memory you
need for other purposes, such as a RAM drive, and give the rest
to SMARTDRV. If you have one or two applications that
require extended memory, you may set up two configurations in
CONFIG.SYS and AUTOEXEC.BAT. When you want to use
one of the applications that needs extended memory, boot with a
smaller cache size. Otherwise, boot with the maximum cache
size.

The maximum cache size that SMARTDRV creates for itself is
2M. If you want a larger cache, you must specify the cache size
in the SMARTDRV command. If you request a larger cache size
than the available room in extended memory, SMARTDRV
adjusts the cache size accordingly.

Determining How Much Memory SMARTDRV Uses

The SMARTDRV program itself (not the cache) loads into
upper memory if possible; otherwise, it loads into conventional
memory. The size of the program depends on the number of
elements it must keep track of and the size of the read-ahead
buffer. With a typical setup of 256 elements and a 16K read-
ahead buffer, SMARTDRV takes about 28K of conventional or
upper memory. With 4,096 elements, it runs to 65K. If you
reduce the read-ahead buffer to 2K, it takes up only 51K.

You can determine how much space your SMARTDRV is taking
up with the MEM /C /P command. If it is using too much
space, and in particular if it is too big to fit into upper memory,
reduce the number of elements or the size of the read-ahead
buffer to reduce the size of the program.

Using a RAM Drive

Another way to avoid disk access is to create and use a RAM
drive. This is a memory area that emulates a disk drive, but with

the access speed of memory. DOS's RAMDRIVE.SYS driver creates and manages a RAM drive. The following command creates a 2M RAM drive in extended memory:

```
DEVICEHIGH=C:\DOS\RAMDRIVE.SYS 2048 /E
```

DOS assigns the next available drive letter to the RAM drive during booting. You will see a message telling you the letter assigned to the RAM drive.

Because RAM drives are in memory, they lose their data when you reboot or shut off the power. You have to load the RAM drive after booting and store any modified data on a hard disk before rebooting or powering down. And you are out of luck if the power goes out. For this reason, you probably do not want to use your RAM drive for programs or data files. But RAM drives are perfect for all those temporary files that DOS and Windows create. And they really help to speed up the Shell, Windows, and DOS commands involving piping. If DOS assigns the letter D to a RAM drive, the following command directs all DOS and Windows temporary files to the RAM drive:

```
SET TEMP=D:\
```

Warning: If you use Windows, do not assign TEMP to any drive, in memory or on disk, with less than 2M of space. Windows needs at least 2M for its temporary print files. If less than 2M is available, Windows scrambles your print data. Keep in mind that DOS uses some of the RAM drive space for the drive's root directory and FAT. A 2M drive loses 6K to the root directory and FAT.

Placing the RAM Drive

If you have extended memory available, by all means place the RAM drive there. If you have only expanded memory available, that is the best choice. If you use EMM386.EXE to emulate expanded memory, your RAM drive will run faster if placed in extended memory instead of emulated expanded memory. If you do not have extended or expanded memory, you probably should not use a RAM drive.

Balancing RAM Drive and the SMARTDRV Cache

If you have a limited amount of extended memory, SMARTDRV gives you more performance improvement than a RAM drive. But if you have at least 4M of extended memory, you have room for both. Make your cache at least 2M. If you do not use Windows, your RAM drive can be smaller than 2M.

14

Working with Your Hardware

DOS includes several utilities to help you make the best use of your hardware. The POWER.EXE driver helps to conserve the batteries in your portable computer. INTERLNK and INTERSVR enable you to connect two computers and access one from the other. DRIVER.SYS assigns alternate names to your floppy drives. MODE enables you to configure your monitor, your keyboard, and your printer. GRAPHICS helps you capture screen prints of graphics screens.

Conserving Battery Power

If you have a battery-operated computer, the POWER.EXE driver reduces power consumption when the computer is turned on but you are not actually doing something. This can help to make your battery charge last longer.

Note: Look up POWER.EXE in DOS's on-screen Help system to see its syntax, notes, and examples.

When you load POWER.EXE, you can specify a power conservation setting of MAX, REG, MIN, or STD. REG is the default. Try MAX first; it gives you the greatest power savings but may interfere with your work. If MAX is not satisfactory, first try REG, and then MIN. If your computer adheres to the Advanced Power Management specification, you also can try the STD setting, which uses your hardware's power-management features.

You do not have to reboot to adjust the power setting. After POWER.EXE has been loaded, the POWER command can change the setting. The following command, for example, changes the power setting to REG, but only if POWER.EXE has been installed:

```
POWER ADV
```

You also can use the POWER command to turn off power management (POWER OFF) and back on again (POWER ON). If you are not sure what the current power setting is, enter **POWER** without any parameters, as follows:

```
POWER

Power Management Status
- - - - - - - - - - - - - - - - - - - - - - -
Setting =  ADV: MAX
CPU: idle 64% of time.
```

This report tells you that the current setting is MAX. It also says that the CPU is idle 64% of the time. POWER reduces power consumption when the CPU is idle.

Linking Two Computers

If you work with a desktop computer at the office and a portable computer in the field, DOS's INTERLNK.EXE driver gives you the capability to physically link the two computers so that you can copy programs and data from one to the other without having to use floppy disks as a go-between. INTERLNK can connect any two computers, whether they are both desktops, both portables, or one of each. As long as they are close enough to be connected by a cable, they can be linked.

When the two computers are linked, one is the *client* and the other is the *server*. You use the keyboard and monitor of the client to access the drives and printer(s) of the server. While the link is in effect, the keyboard and monitor of the server are inactive. INTERLNK redirects the server's drives to look like they belong to the client. If each computer has two floppy drives and one hard drive, for example, the client can access its own drives by the names A, B, and C, as usual; it also has access to drives D, E, and F, which represent the server's drives A, B, and C. It can apply many commands to those drives that it applies to its own drives A, B, and C. The client can move or copy data from drive C to drive F, it can run a program located on drive F, and so on.

> **Note:** Commands that affect the drive's basic layout, such as FORMAT and DEFRAG, cannot be applied to the server drives.

INTERLNK appeared with DOS 6 but it does not require DOS 6. You can copy and use the INTERLNK programs on any computer that is running DOS 3 or later. So you can connect your DOS 6 system to a computer that is using DOS 5. INTERLNK includes an /RCOPY function to copy the appropriate programs to the other computer, but frankly, it is easier to transfer them by disk (unless the two computers don't have compatible floppy drives).

Making the Connection

You connect the two computers by their serial ports or their parallel ports. If you want to use serial ports, you must use a 3-wire serial cable or a 7-wire null-modem cable. To connect their parallel ports, you must use a bidirectional parallel cable.

Installing INTERSVR and Redirecting Drives

> **Note:** Look up INTERSVR in DOS's on-screen Help system to see its syntax, notes, and examples.

You must install the INTERSVR program on the server computer and the INTERLNK.EXE driver on the client computer. Install INTERSVR with an INTERSVR command. If you do not specify drive redirection, INTERSVR redirects all the server's local hard, floppy, and RAM drives. (It does not redirect network or CD-ROM drives.) You probably do not need to access the server's floppy drives (unless you need to read or write some floppies that do not fit the client computer's drives). You can override the default redirection by specifying the drives to be redirected or the drives to be omitted, whichever you find most convenient. The following command loads

INTERSVR and redirects only drive C:

```
INTERSVR C:
```

While INTERSVR is loaded, the INTERSVR window appears on the server's screen and you cannot use the computer for anything else (see fig. 14.1). Press Alt+F4 on the server computer's keyboard when you are ready to break the connection and unload INTERSVR.

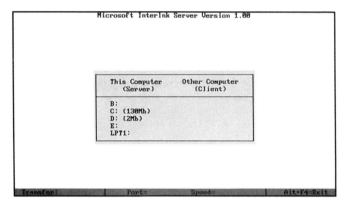

Figure 14.1. *The INTERSVR window identifies the server's redirected ports; the client column is filled in when INTERLNK is loaded on the client computer.*

Identifying the Connecting Port

If you do not specify the connecting port, INTERSVR scans all the server's serial and parallel ports looking for the connection. This can have detrimental effects. First, it causes INTERSVR to load software to handle both serial and parallel ports, which takes up more memory space. More important, if you have a mouse attached to a serial port, the scanning process can interfere with the mouse driver. To avoid these effects, you are best off specifying the connecting port. The following command loads INTERSVR, excludes the floppy drives, and identifies COM2 as the connecting port:

```
INTERSVR /X:A /X:B /COM2
```

Setting the Baud Rate

INTERLNK and INTERSVR can transfer data at 115,200 baud. If that turns out to be too fast for your system, you can request a slower baud rate with the /BAUD parameter. If your computers hang up when you install INTERLNK or INTERSVR, reboot and try the /V switch.

Installing INTERLNK

Note: Look up INTERLNK.EXE in DOS's on-screen Help system to see its syntax, notes, and examples.

Install INTERLNK.EXE on the client computer from CONFIG.SYS. Notice that you can specify the number of drives to be redirected. The default is three, but you can specify more or less as needed. Suppose that the server has two floppy drives, two hard drives, and a RAM drive, and the INTERSVR command did not specify or omit any drives. If INTERLNK redirects only three drives, only the server's drives A, B, and C are redirected. If you want to redirect the server's drives C, D, and E instead, you must set up the INTERSVR command accordingly.

Delaying the Connection

Sometimes you install INTERLNK during booting but do not really expect to establish the connection until later. You can use the /NOSCAN switch to tell INTERLNK not to scan the ports at this time. Then you must use the INTERLNK command to finalize the connection, as explained later in this chapter.

Using the /AUTO Switch

Suppose that you have a laptop and you will be using INTERLNK often to transfer data to your desktop. You do not want to take up valuable memory space with INTERLNK when you are not going to use it. But it is a pain to edit CONFIG.SYS every time you want to load it. You can set CONFIG.SYS up with configuration blocks so that you can choose when to load INTERLNK.EXE. But there is an easier way. The INTERLNK.EXE command includes an /AUTO switch that suppresses the loading of INTERLNK.EXE unless the connection can be established. If INTERLNK.EXE cannot find a cable or if the connected computer is not yet in server mode, it does not load.

When you use the /AUTO switch and you want to load INTERLNK.EXE, install INTERSVR on the server computer, cable the two computers together, and then reboot the client computer to load the device driver.

Coordinating INTERLNK with INTERSVR

If you used the /BAUD parameter or the /V switch on the INTERSVR command, you also need them when you install the INTERLNK driver.

Finalizing the Connection

> **Note:** Look up INTERLNK in DOS's on-screen Help system to see its syntax, notes, and examples.

If you loaded INTERLNK.EXE before the two computers were linked and INTERSVR was installed on the server computer, INTERLNK could not make the connection. When the server computer is ready and the cable is hooked up, use the INTERLNK command to make the connection.

You also can use the INTERLNK command to override the default drive assignments. You cannot access different server drives, but you can change the way the names are assigned. Suppose that the current assignments look like this:

```
This Computer                Other Computer
   (Client)                      (Server)
   - - - - - -                   - - - - - - -
        E:           equals          C:
        F:           equals          D:
        G:           equals          E:
```

Suppose, instead, that you want to refer to drive E as E and drive D as F, and you want to drop the connection with drive C. The following command reassigns the drive names:

```
INTERLNK E:=E: F:=D: G:=
```

Assigning Additional Names to Your Drives

If you have only one floppy drive, it is assigned two names, A and B. To copy a file from one floppy to another, you can use a command like this:

```
COPY A:TENNIS.DAT B:
```

DOS tells you when to install the floppy disk that represents drive A and when to install the disk that represents drive B.

If you have two floppy drives of the same type, there is no problem copying files from one floppy disk to the other. Put one disk in drive A and the other in drive B and use the same command shown previously.

But what if you have two different size drives, as so many people do? How do you copy a file from one floppy to another of the same size? Ordinarily, you cannot do it in one command. You have to copy the file to another drive, change floppies, and copy it back. But the DRIVER.SYS driver enables you to assign two names to the same floppy drive so that you can copy files in one command.

Note: Look up DRIVER.SYS in DOS's on-screen Help system to see its syntax, notes, and examples.

When you load DRIVER.SYS, you must identify the drive for which you are requesting a name by using the /D:*n* parameter. If you want a second name for drive A, specify /D:0. For drive B, specify /D:1. If you have external floppies in addition to drives A and B, the third floppy drive is /D:2, and so on. You do not need any other parameters if all you are doing is requesting an additional drive name.

The following command loads DRIVER.SYS to assign a second drive name to drive A:

```
DEVICEHIGH=C:\DOS\DRIVER.SYS /D:0
```

If you also want a second name for drive B, you must specify another DEVICE command to load another copy of DRIVER.SYS for /D:1.

When DRIVER.SYS is installed, you will see a message similar
to the following:

```
Loaded External Disk Driver for Drive E
```

Do not miss this message; it tells you the alternate name assigned
to your drive. You also can see the alternate name in DOS Shell's
drive list.

The alternate name could cause some of your other drives that
are created by drivers in CONFIG.SYS or AUTOEXEC.BAT,
such as a RAM drive or a CD-ROM drive, to have their names
changed. You may have to rewrite some of your batch programs
and change your SET TEMP= command to accommodate the
drive name changes.

Specifying the Last Drive Name

DOS does not have an unlimited number of drive names
available. By default, it either makes five drive names available (A
through E) or one drive name for each physical drive—whichever is larger. If you have only three drives, two more drive
names are available and DRIVER.SYS can use them as alternate
drive names. But if you have two floppies, one hard drive, one
CD-ROM drive, and one RAM drive, there are no extra drive
names available and DRIVER.SYS displays the message Out of
drive names.

You can make more drive names available by specifying the
LASTDRIVE command in CONFIG.SYS. If, for example, you
need seven drive names, include LASTDRIVE=G in
CONFIG.SYS.

Configuring Your Console Device

Your monitor may be capable of display modes other than the
default. You may be able to display 43 or 50 lines per screen
instead of the default 25, for example, and you may be able to
display 40 characters per line instead of the default 80. You must
install ANSI.SYS as explained in Chapter 2 to reset the lines per
screen.

Note: Look up MODE (set display mode) in DOS's on-screen Help system to see its syntax, notes, and examples.

Displaying 43 or 50 lines per screen enables you to see more information at once. The following command causes DOS to display 43 lines per screen:

```
MODE CON LINES=43
```

Displaying only 40 characters per line makes the characters much larger and easier to see, although many messages and reports are more than 40 characters long. There are several ways to request 40 characters per line:

```
MODE 40
MODE COLS=40
MODE CON COLS=40
MODE CO40
MODE BW40
```

You can use comparable commands to switch back to 80 characters per line. Changes to your video device usually affect the DOS command screen only; most applications control the monitor themselves.

Configuring Your Keyboard

Note: Look up MODE (set typematic rate) to see the MODE command syntax, notes, and examples for configuring the keyboard.

When you hold down a key on your keyboard for a moment, it begins to repeat. This is called the *typematic* feature, and you can control both the delay before it begins repeating and the rate at which it repeats. For some people, the default rate is too fast. When they hold down the backspace key to delete a string of characters, for example, they end up deleting more characters than they want to.

When you are setting the typematic rate, you must specify the CON parameter and you must specify RATE= and DELAY=. The following command sets the typematic rate to approximately five characters per second and the delay to a half second:

```
MODE CON RATE=5 DELAY=2
```

Configuring Your Printers

> **Note:** Look up MODE (configure printer) to see the MODE syntax, notes, and examples for configuring the printer.

When you print using an application, such as a word processor, the application probably provides a device driver that controls font, spacing, and so on. But when you print straight through DOS, as when you redirect something to LPT1 or PRN, you have very few choices. With many IBM- or Epson-compatible printers, however, you can determine whether you want 6 or 8 lines per inch and 80 or 132 characters per line. The following commands, for example, make the print as small as possible so that you can print more per information per page:

```
MODE LPT1 132,8
MODE LPT1 COLS=132 LINES=8
```

> **Note:** Look up MODE (configure serial port) to see the MODE syntax, notes, and examples for specifying serial port parameters.

When you want to use any serial device, DOS must know what serial parameters (baud rate, and so on) to use with the device. With mice and modems, you usually use a driver that controls the serial parameters. But with a serial printer, you may need to set the parameters through DOS. The following two commands both have the same effect. They set up COM1 for 9600 baud, no parity, eight data bits, and one stop bit:

```
MODE COM1 96,N,8,1
MODE COM1 BAUD=96 PARITY=N DATA=8 STOP=1
```

Note: If you specify a retry parameter for the parallel printer or the serial port, a small resident portion of the MODE program is loaded. There is no way to load this TSR into upper memory.

Making a Serial Printer Your Main DOS Printer

Note: Look up MODE (redirect printing) to see the MODE syntax, notes, and examples to redirect a parallel printer to a serial printer.

DOS uses the printer attached to LPT1 as the target for screen prints, echo printing, data redirected to PRN, and the default target of the PRINT command. If your only printer is a serial printer, you need to redirect LPT1 to it. The following command redirects all data sent to LPT1 to COM1:

```
MODE LPT1=COM1
```

This command must follow the command that sets the serial port parameters for COM1.

Viewing MODE Settings

You can see all your MODE settings by entering MODE without any parameters, which produces a report something like this:

```
Status for device LPT1:
-----------------------------------------------------
LPT1: rerouted to COM1:
Retry=NONE

Code page operation not supported on this device
```

```
Status for device LPT2:
- - - - - - - - - - - - - - - - - - - - - - - - - - - - - - - - - - - - - - - - - - - - - - - - - - - -
LPT2: not rerouted

Status for device LPT3:
- - - - - - - - - - - - - - - - - - - - - - - - - - - - - - - - - - - - - - - - - - - - - - - - - - - -
LPT3: not rerouted

Status for device CON:
- - - - - - - - - - - - - - - - - - - - - - - - - - - - - - - - - - - - - - - - - - - - - - - - - - - -
Columns=80
Lines=25

Code page operation not supported on this device

Status for device COM1:
- - - - - - - - - - - - - - - - - - - - - - - - - - - - - - - - - - - - - - - - - - - - - - - - - - - -
Retry=B
```

If you want to see the status for just one device, include the device name in the MODE command with no other parameters. The following command displays a status report for COM1:

```
MODE COM1
```

But if you want to see the status of a parallel port, you must use the /STATUS switch. Without any other parameters, MODE LPT*n* undoes any redirection for the specified parallel port. The following command reports on the status of LPT1 as shown in the sample report that follows it:

```
MODE LPT1 /STATUS
```

```
Status for device LPT1:
- - - - - - - - - - - - - - - - - - - - - - - - - - - - - - - - - - - - - - - - - - - - - - - - - - - -
LPT1: not rerouted
Retry=NONE

Code page operation not supported on this device
```

Whereas the following command undoes any redirection of LPT1, as shown in the message that follows it:

```
MODE LPT1
```

```
LPT1: not rerouted

No retry on parallel printer time-out
```

Capturing Screen Prints

Note: Look up GRAPHICS in DOS's on-screen Help system to see its syntax, notes, and examples.

By default, DOS can respond to the Print Screen key only when the screen is in text mode. It easily can print the command prompt screen, for example. It can print the DOS Shell screen only if it is set to text mode. If you want to be able to capture graphics screens to print using only the facilities provided by DOS, you must install the GRAPHICS TSR. Suppose that you have a Hewlett-Packard Deskjet printer. The following command enables DOS to capture graphics screen prints on your printer (the LOADHIGH prefix loads it into upper memory if possible):

```
LOADHIGH GRAPHICS DESKJET
```

GRAPHICS normally reverses the colors of the monochrome screen so that the command prompt screen prints black characters on a white background. Include the /R switch if you prefer the screen prints to have the same colors as the screen. For color printers, use the /B switch to request a color background instead of white.

The aspect ratio determines the ratio of the horizontal dimension to the vertical dimension. GRAPHICS attempts to select the correct aspect ratio for your printer. But if circles print as ellipses and squares print as rectangles, try /PB:STD or /PB:LCD. One of them may fix the problem.

The GRAPHICS command does not work with all printers and all monitors, but it works with the standard ones. It also does not work with many applications, but it does work with the DOS Shell screen in graphics mode. If you find that you cannot capture the screen prints that you want using GRAPHICS, you will need a screen-capturing facility such as Collage Plus or HotShot Graphics.

Index